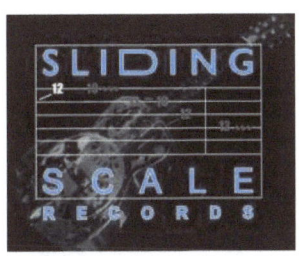

slidingscale.co.uk

Cricut & Construct #1

Miniature paper flowers for cutting machines

Angie Scarr & Frank Fisher

Dedication

Dedicated to all my Patreon patrons, both those who are listed on the thanks page and the anonymous ones. Without you this book would never have seen the light of day. Thank you

Publishing Data

First edition published 2022 (SSPB14)

Text copyright Angie Scarr and Frank Fisher

Illustration, composites and photographs copyright Frank Fisher, Angie Scarr

Design by Frank Fisher, Angie Scarr

Plaza De Andalucía 1, Campofrío, 21668, Huelva, Spain.

ISBN 9788412602319

All rights reserved. No part of this book may be reproduced, or transmitted in any form or by any means without the express permission of the copyright owners.

The right of Angie Scarr and Frank Fisher to be identified as the author of this work has been asserted in accordance with the Copyright Designs and Patents Act 1988, sections 77 & 78.

No part of this publication may be reproduced, stored in a retrieval system or transmitted in any form or by any means without the prior permission of the publisher and author or her agents.

Descriptions of sales and advertising platforms are for information purposes only and are not recommendations. The authors can accept no responsibility for the application of any information contained in this book. Further, no responsibility is implied or accepted for current or future application of social media and data collection laws.

The publishers and author can accept no legal responsibility for any consequences from the application of information instructions or advice given in this publication.

Contents

Intro, tools & technique	9
Tools and materials used in this book	10
Using non-recommended items	12
Copyright issues	12
General cutting advice for miniature floral elements	13
General principles of design for miniatures using Cricut and other cutters	13
My way of working	13
Analysing	14
Why I use vellum	16
Flower painting techniques	17
Simple flowers & leaves	21
Filler plants & leaves	22
Bird of paradise	25
Sunflower	26
Gerbera, ox eye daisy and echinacea	29
Summer flowers	31
Wildflowers	32
Dahlia	33
Carnation and African marigold	34
Roses	36
Freesias	38
Gladioli	40
Xmas flowers and plants	43
Hellebore	44
Holly	44
Mistletoe	45
Poinsettia	45
Spring flowers	47
Primroses and violets	48
Daffodils	50
Crocus	51
Cyclamen	52
Bluebells	53
Snowdrops	53
Iris	55
Exotic and tropical plants	57
Swiss cheese plants (exotic 'holey' leaves)	58
Acer bush	59
Printing - prayer plants etc.	60
Orchids 3 styles	61
Display items for your scene	63
Plant pots, buckets and tall tubs or vases	64
Problem solver	68
We asked Lisa for common issues	70
Mix and match	70
Supplies	71
Biography	72
Thanks and acknowledgements	72
Patreon - why I love my patrons	73
Other books by Sliding Scale	74
Our website	75
Bundled offers at our Etsy shop	76

Intro, tools & technique

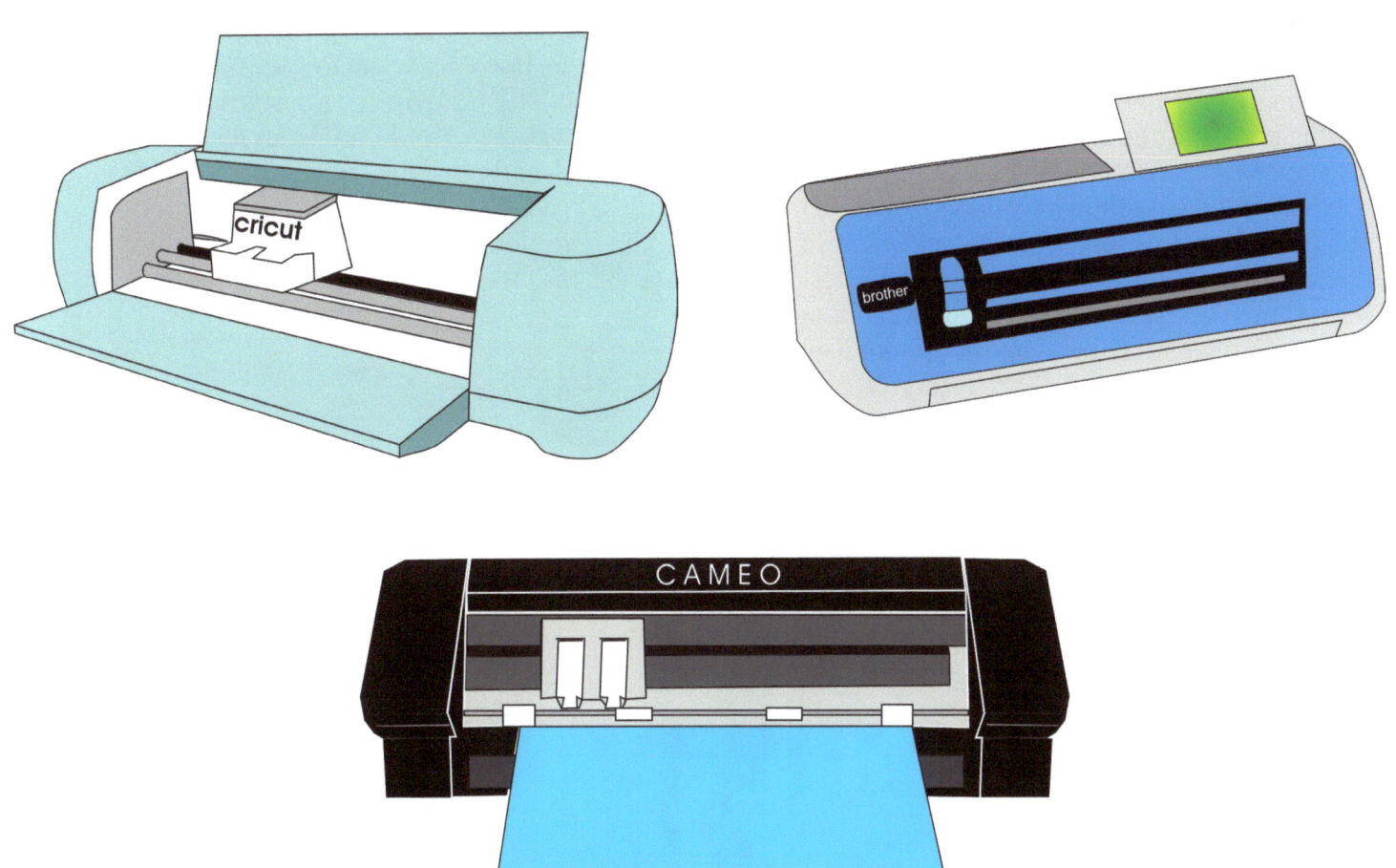

In this book ...

This book does not cover how to set up and use a Cricut or Silhouette machine right out of the box. It is intended for those who already know their machine and how it works. If you are a new owner who is also a miniaturist I recommend Lisa Sones Peck's book Making Miniatures With A Cricut Maker. There are also loads of support groups on facebook and lots of videos on Youtube which tell you how to set up your machines.

This book can be used by those wishing to purchase the design bundles on Etsy and those hoping to make their own designs. If you are purchasing the design bundle initially you can skip the design principles part and come back to it if you do decide to design your own flowers etc. later.

I can say straight off that almost as soon as this book hits the market it will be out of date because the machine manufacturers do like to change the way things work regularly. Is this to improve, to keep you on your toes or to lock people into using their software, their designs and their consumables? We couldn't possibly say. But you may have to ask current users what are the recent changes to the software programs.

Well now you'll know this book is not endorsed by either of the machine manufacturers when we tell you that if you need to change your blades or your mats regularly as we do you may also need to look at cheaper versions. No, the machine manufacturers won't like that, but there you go, I've said it. It's not so different from the situation with print consumables. If you can afford it … get the manufacturer's recommendation. If you can't then do what you need to, to fully succeed and enjoy the process.

Tools and materials used in this book

During the whole of the design stage of the plants in this book we used an old (second hand) Silhouette Cameo. The designs have also been tested by third parties on the Cricut Maker. The earlier Cameos like ours will not handle the heavier cards so Silhouette users may have to double up if using lighter weight materials for the stall/shop constructions.

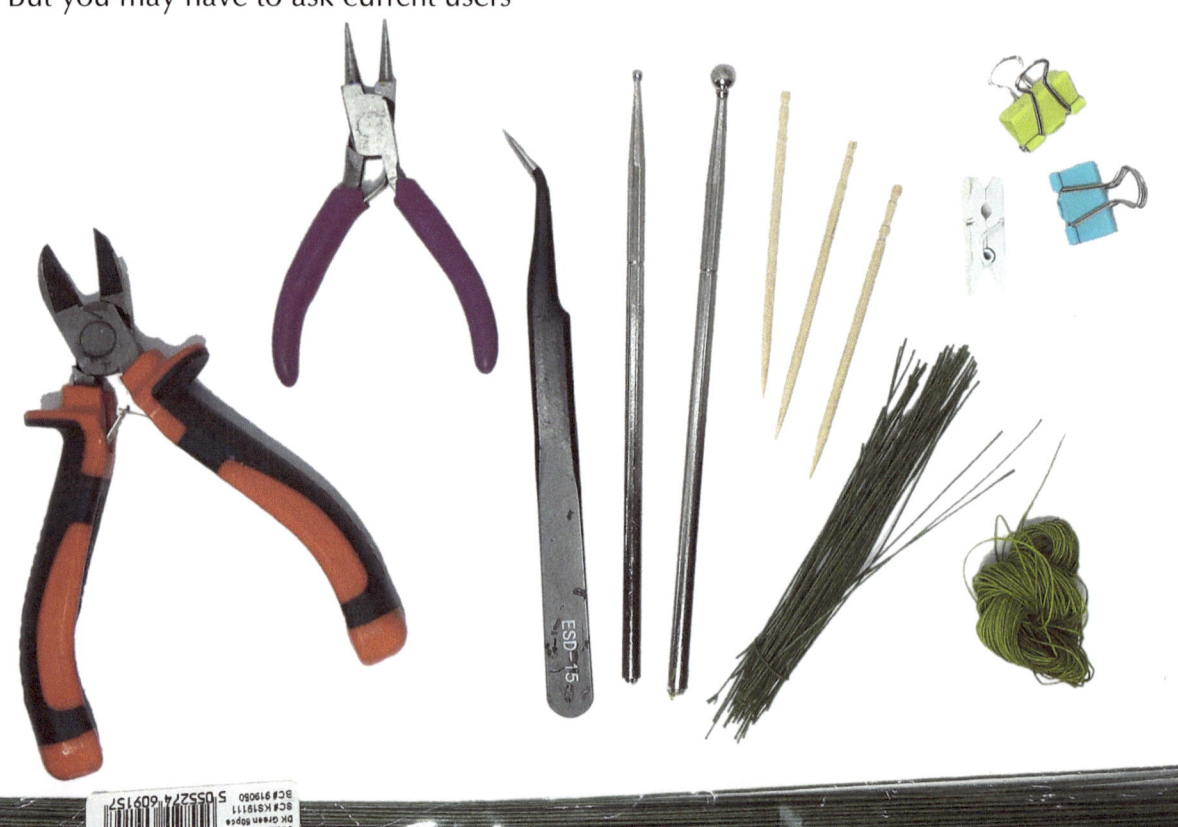

Paper and card

Personally I'm very fond of vellum for both the flowers and leaves. Vellum, similar to tracing paper and also known as papel de cebolla in Spain, is very popular among the scrapbooking fraternity. It comes in several weights. We tend to use 110gsm/50lb for lightweight petals and leaves and 160gsm/75lb for heavier weight leaves.

Card for the crates, window boxes and stand

Be aware that some card leaves residue on your mats. Because of the number of types available we can't give specific advice. Of course the ones recommended by your machine company are likely to extend the life of your mat. I advise you to use an old mat that still has one good edge to check out small squares of any new card you are thinking of using. Then hold the mat up to the light to see if the residue has 'dulled' the surface.

If your mat has too strong a grip, dab it gently with a clean cloth or T shirt. The glue will take up tiny particles from the fabric and this will make it a little less strong.

Paint

We use Ecoline artists inks for the most part for the plants. I added opaque matte white acrylic for mixing lighter more opaque colours. I use some little ceramic bowls for dip-dying petals and leaves and a plastic art palette for smaller quantities or colour mixes.

- Kitchen roll for drying petals and leaves
- I also use matte acrylic paints for the stalls and coloured crates
- Fast tacky PVA glue in a small nozzle (precise application) bottle. PVA glue can also be mixed with paints or powders for different 3D effects such as berries and pistils
- Flocking powder, pearlised powder and even heat expanding powders have their uses
- Finely snipped cotton or silk threads for stamens and stigmas.
- A pair of wire cutters
- Small needle nose pliers
- Fine pointed jewellers tweezers
- Ball tools of different sizes
- Cocktail sticks
- Paper coated flower wire sizes 26 to 32 and, if you can find it, ultra fine beading wire
- Very fine paper cord is useful but optional as it can be difficult to find. See suppliers in the back of the book
- Craft clothes pegs or small clips
- No hole beads for berries
- Cotton or silk thread for flower centres.
- EVA foam. Sometimes called flower shaping foam. Not to be confused with Oasis
- Oasis type dry flower foam used for standing flowers in for storage of work in progress, I use boxes filled with Oasis dry flower foam

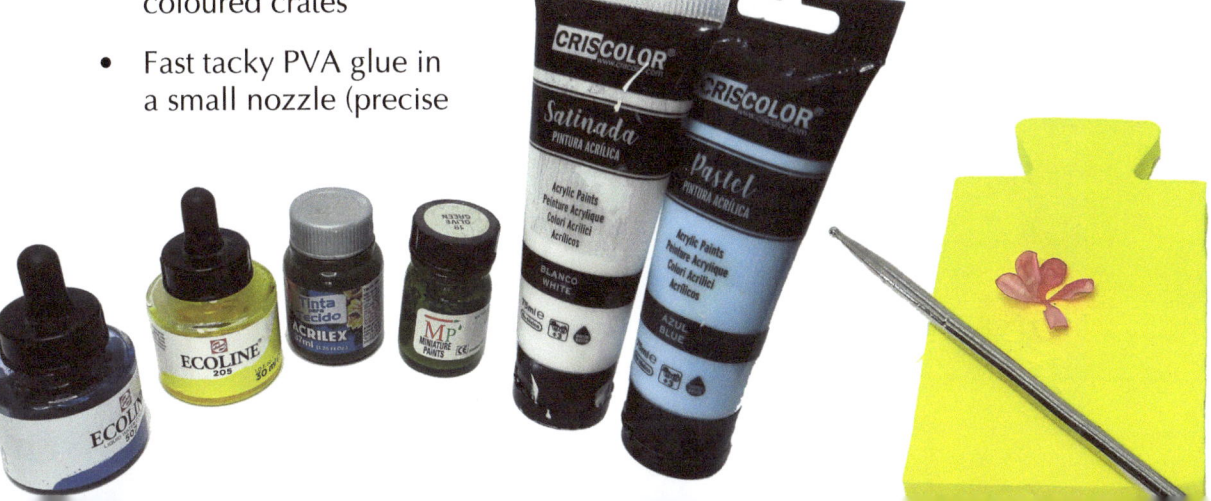

Using Non-recommended items

Of course the machine companies want you to buy their designs and their consumables like blades mats and the like. If you use them you will be more likely to get predictable results, however some of us have to find alternative consumable items because of price or availability. When you do this of course the results can be unexpected. A mat may not stick in a way you are used to. Or a blade may be weaker, or cut deeper than you expect.

When it comes to designs many of us really don't want to be constrained to the designs attached to the design software of our machine. The machine companies seem to make it more and more difficult for them to be recognised and sized correctly by the machine software. There is little you can do to stop your design software updating with these little 'bugs' embedded in them. All designers are aware of this so if you are buying 3rd party designs and they don't work for you you will need to contact the designer/vendor to ask for whatever the 'fix' for that week is! It can be a bit of a game of cat and mouse. If you want your results to be wholly predictable buy the manufacturers consumables and designs. If you want more creative freedom you have to take a little pain.

Copyright issues

The designs used in this book are our designs and are copyright. You might decide to use our designs or your own or a mixture of both. There are just a few simple rules when designing your own work.

In my case, I am happy for people to cut as many items from purchased designs as they like, work on them and sell their own work. BUT don't copy mine or other people's design work if you are going to sell your designs. Of course a flower is a flower and there really won't be much difference between your daisy and anyone else's daisy however copies are obvious by the exact petal shaping and number of petals and how they are connected on each layer etc. Make sure you work from zero if you are making your own copyrighted designs for sale as designs. It is simply more artistic and morally right to do so.

So, your choice is making your own designs or using paid for and free SVGS etc.

General cutting advice for miniature floral elements

Imperfect grip and a dull blade will make it really difficult to get good cuts in miniature.

Ensure your blade tip is clean and in good condition to avoid snagging. Gluey or broken blades will result in tearing and lifting of the paper/vellum. This is especially important for very fine or complex shapes.

Also make sure your mat is in good condition and that you use a roller to adhere the vellum or paper to the mat. Ensure there are no bubbles of air under the map nor lifting due to damp or warped paper or card. Vellum leaves less residue on the mat. Painting your elements while still on the mat can leave paint on the mat

Elements should be designed to be as snag free as possible (see later in this section) but due to their tiny size and complexity any problems with glue on a blade or bluntness or poor adhesion to your mat will result in some pieces snagging. So make sure that your designs bear in mind the machine's limitations AND the limitations of your materials and semi-consumables such as mats and blades. When cutting miniatures it can be a little heavy on both blades and mats so try to take advice on some of the materials you want to use before ruining too many mats.

Expect very complex shapes like the palm fern to take quite a long time to cut. Simpler shapes can be really quick.

General principles of design for miniatures using Cricut and other cutters

My way of working

Most people just say "I could never do that" as if it were really a skill. But it isn't. It's just having the patience to take things one step at a time. So that's what all my books are about and this one is no different.

The way I work is about giving people a peek into my own mind and way of problem solving. Making people LOOK at stuff and believe that in order to make amazing things you only have to have a problem…and then solve it. Most people just see stuff and imagine they know what they are looking at (this includes me!) We think we know what colour we are looking at without ever analysing. We almost imagine the shape and the colour and think we can work from memory. We can't! Have you seen some of the greens people make for leaves in miniature for example? They never compare with the real thing. My best advice to you is to really look at the item you would like to make and to take it apart into its size, shape, colour etc. And then look at what it is about it that you like or don't like. Copy the things you like and remove the things you don't like. And in miniature exaggerate the elements which make up the 'essence' of the thing.

You will see on some of the first pages of a project my little 'scribbles'. The general outline, shapes etc. of things and sometimes I'll write notes on how they go together.

Analysing

Use a graphics program like inkscape which is free and runs on Mac, Linux and Windows. We use Corel Draw but we're old! You can stay within the design software of your machine but we find that restrictive.

In our case Frank and I work as a team. I choose the plants and draw how I think they should be constructed, in how many layers, whether petals or leaves are joined and how.

Firstly I look at photographs on the internet unless I have one of the flowers or plants at home, which is obviously my favourite way of working. Sometimes I will throw a printout of a photo at him, draw on them and make notes on the sides. I can't share those photographs because of copyright. You can't necessarily copy shapes from a photograph because you have to remember that 3 dimensional curves shorten how petals and leaves look in a 2 dimensional image, for example. You have to have a real 'feel' for nature to recognise the type of curve in a leaf or petal. Our early work was definitely a bit clunky until Frank learned my obsession with natural curves and I learned the limits of what his software could do. Sometimes I had to reassure him that the extra work was worth it on a particularly tricky shape. Digital drawing programs might make this process much easier but us old folks have yet to get to grips with them!

Examine the plants. How each part connects and where. We can all imagine that we know what a plant looks like, guess its size, or how it goes together but there is absolutely no better way than through careful observation

Here I dissect a hibiscus and scan it. If you don't have a scanner you can take a photo and use your graphics programme to actually draw round the photo on your screen.

Whether the pictures show a shape in a 'skewed' angle, for example petals can often be longer and connect further back than we imagine. They may then be curled outwards.

Hibiscus plant dissected

Then you have to work out how long YOU need to make them. Work out whether you will need to put a hole in a bunch of connected petals to pass a stem through or whether you can connect the stem directly. Can the stem double up as a pistil for example? Or if you can make a loop or bend to connect petals to the wire or to each other with the wire in between. This will affect how you design your plant. Will you divide the petals up into layers or do them all in one?

This hibiscus has overlapping petals. Of course you can create layers to make overlaps but if the flower is formed in a trumpet shape, the petals will naturally overlap as they come up the stem so in this case I dissected the flower to copy its actual shape. This is pretty easy for a large flower like hibiscus but for a tiny flower like jasmine you are better off designing a tiny blossom shape and simply adding some glue to the back to make it look like the tiny trumpet.

Note the veins on the petal and whether they are visible both inside and outside of the flower. This will help you make both open and closed flowers. When we scanned the petals we realised we could make them all from one very open flower as the lower part of each of the petals forms a trumpet

There are 2 types of Calyx on each hibiscus flower.

In many cases you can't simply size-down larger designs that you may have found in a file bundle because you may need to simplify a design for strength and ease of cutting.

To successfully design the very smallest, most delicate items in miniature there are a few things you have to remember since we are working at the very limits of what these machines can do.

We found really early on, that you simply can't have sharp V shaped internal bends on any of your designs because the machine is very good at swivelling round really small curves but not changing direction instantly. You will see that our designs have curves on all internal joints. This is to enable the blade to swivel gently rather than getting stuck on one point where it has then to go back against itself. Having internal sharp corners almost always results in tears (torn paper) and tears (boo hoo). The smoother your changes in direction the smoother your machine is going to work. That

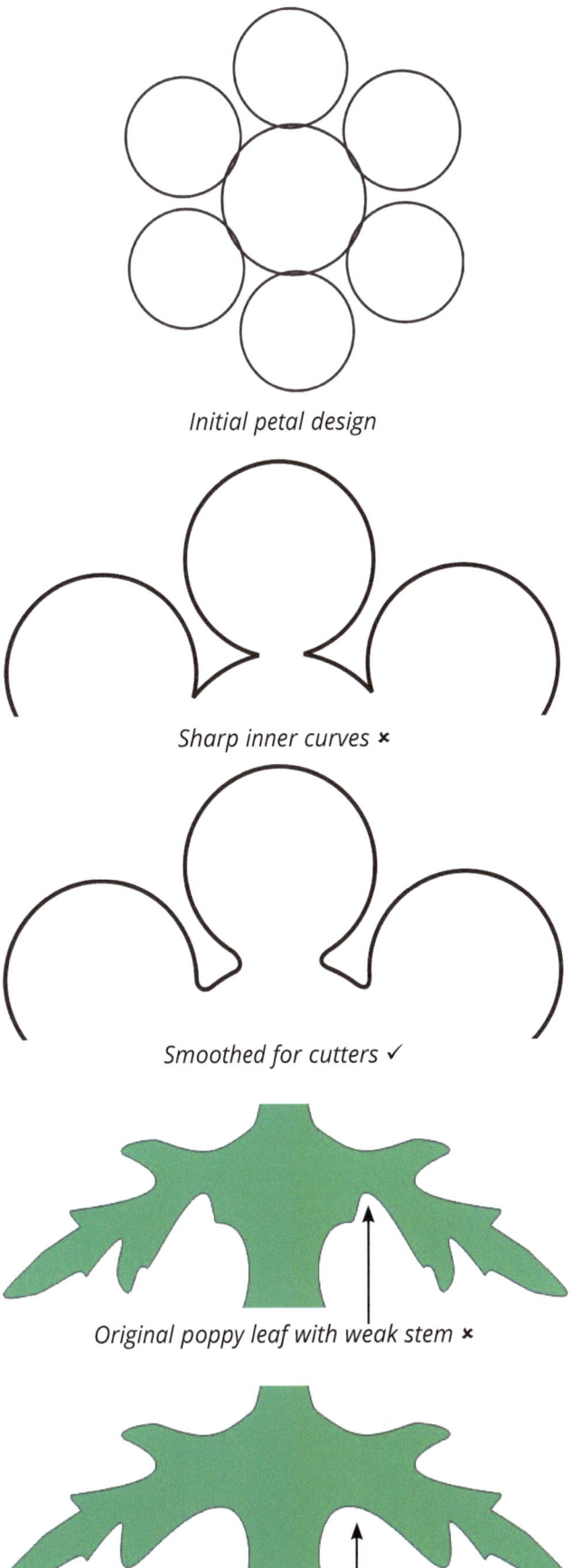

Initial petal design

Sharp inner curves ✗

Smoothed for cutters ✓

Original poppy leaf with weak stem ✗

Smoothed for cutters ✓

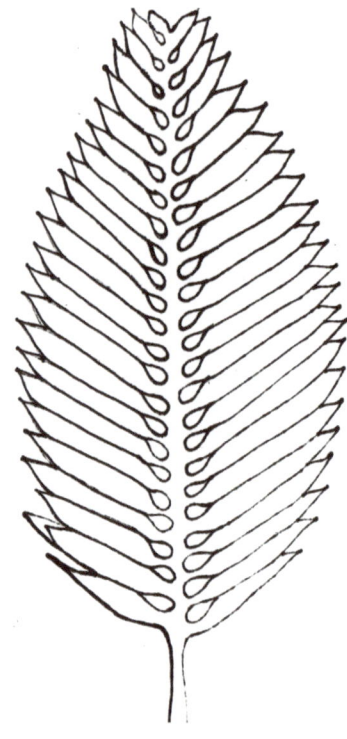

My design with exaggerated rounding

said, you should minimise the data points. The more your machine has to 'change direction' the longer the cut will take.

Here is one of my trickier design challenges where I had to design smooth curves between every one of the leaflets in a palm fern frond.

When you have tried your first cut you may see a place where your design is weak. As you can see on our first design for poppy leaves. A complex little design which we simplified from a photo of a real leaf. When we cut this one we found it regularly tore in the little nodes on the bottom leaves so we smoothed that round to a curve. Half the fun of designing is learning what the machine will and will not do. At first it can be very frustrating but eventually you realise what the limitations of the machine are, you'll find you start to design intuitively with the machine in mind. little curve always helps the machine to 'glide'.

Why I use vellum

Vellum sticks well to your mat and leaves little to no residue. Cuts cleanly as long as your blade is fresh, and paints well to make a really translucent finish.

Coloured vellum

Drawbacks can be that it can be too translucent especially on the leaves. This means you have to get a really thick layer of colour on. Using a more opaque paint can help but then leaves a thicker layer reducing the delicacy of your work.

The other drawback of vellum is that it can 'crack' and tear at weak points when removing from mats. Especially if your mat is really sticky. Very fine petal or leaf joints are prone to tearing because of this. If you take care that none of your joins between petals and centres to flowers are weakened by being sharp angles you can minimise this problem. If it still happens you should try using a lighter adhesive mat.

Vellum comes in various weights and colours. I usually use the translucent (white) one at 110gsm /50lb.

Paper

The benefits of using paper are more opacity (This can be a drawback on delicate petals but a benefit on more opaque leaves) paper is easier to cut too but also tears very easily. Paper also tends to leave more residue on your cutting mat.

Flower painting techniques

I most often use Ecoline inks but they are very translucent and not very concentrated. If you wish to concentrate them in your work you can leave them in a bowl to dry before adding more to get a stronger colour or you can dip or paint twice or leave your paper/vellum in the paint for longer. Dipping works best on vellum as it can make paper a little soggy.

You can use water colours or acrylic colours etc. too but remember a heavy base (as in acrylics) will add real and visual weight to your work.

Dip painting
My favourite technique. It's a speedy and successful colouring method and works very well on vellum. Dip both sides as quickly as you can so that the paper doesn't curl too dramatically.

Double colour dip
This way you can add a second blending colour.

Dip with tip smearing
This is when you drag the tip of your freshly dipped petal/leaf along a different or stronger colour. Often along the dried paint on the edge of your bowl or over a watercolour block.

(I did this on the tips of my bird of paradise)

Painting on the cutting mat
This can be a speedy way of getting all your leaves and petals painted but does have a couple of drawbacks.

The risk of getting paint on to your cutting mat, and the fact you can only cover one side of the

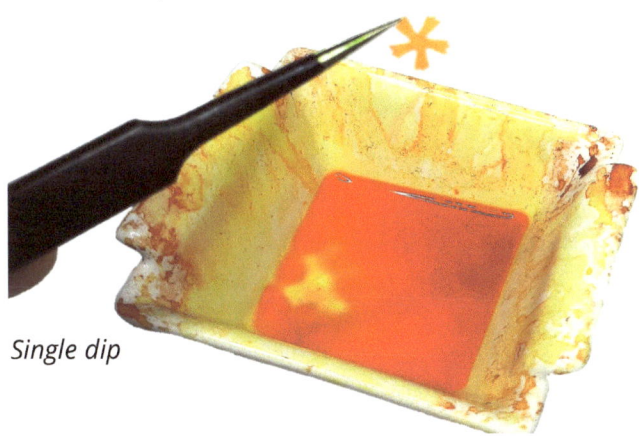

Single dip

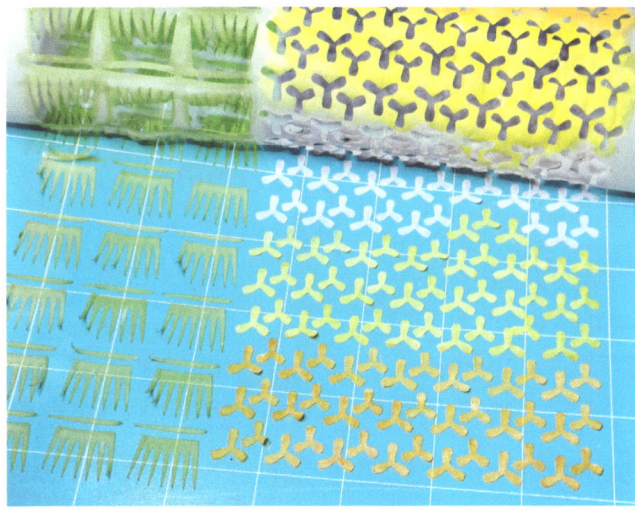

Painting on the mat

Double dip

paper. Then you have to paint the other side. It's useful if you are doing a plant which has different colours on each side of a leaf or petal.

Painting before removing from the mat makes a lovely outlined effect and also helps you to 'weed' the tiny flowers and leaves from the rest of the paper.

Flooding the edges in a different colour
This can be a lovely effect both to exaggerate the edges and in flowers and leaves that do have other colours on edges.

Surface painting
Obviously if you want complex colours and patterns you are going to have to let the painter in you out!

Drawing with fountain pens
It's important that whatever ink you choose isn't permanent for most jobs. This is because you want the colours to 'bleed' for subtle colour ways although some veining in flowers etc. wants to be strong. You just layer those as the top layer or use a permanent ink in that case. You might want to use an artist's fixative spray on the finished work but unless you expect your work to get wet it isn't necessary.

Using the paint to cause curl
I do this mostly with leaves. Fold and score leaves, then use the water in your paint deliberately to to cause curl painting in layers. For different effects, leave the score line (central vein) unpainted or allow more or less paint to lie in the crease.

Masking
You can use watercolour artists masking fluid to mask out previously painted lighter colours before painting or dipping in darker colours. Use a fine tipped masking applicator pen with a darker colour, not white or cream as it can be difficult to see (mine is blue).

One way is to dip paint and then mask and dip again. Or you can mask lighter lines on the cutting mat before painting or before removing and dipping. You can mask centres or edges where the colour is otherwise difficult to paint straight or is too small for example Spider plant or coleus.

Cyclamen with masked leaves

Leaf veins drawn then "washed" with colour

Fountain pen and coloured ink
You can draw the finest of designs on petals and leaves using a fountain pen. Draw in strong colours and leave to dry before washing over with other colours. This gives a really subtle effect of veins on leaves and veining in flowers. See Sunflower leaves. For a stronger vein or spots etc. you can draw over the base colours.

Batch painting/dipping leaves
I tend to do all my leaves in a big batch BUT don't forget not all leaves are the same shade of green so check out whether you need a light, spring green, a deep summer green, a dark green or even a bluish green. One of the most common mistakes miniaturists make is selecting the wrong green. Of course greens do change throughout the year and depending

how fresh your flowers and plants are or how well fertilised. But there are some greens which will always look wrong and somewhat unreal. Do avoid those greens that are just called 'green' and mix your own if a true leaf green isn't available. If using inks a good rule of thumb is to use a lemon yellow and an almost indigo blue at about 10-1 for a spring green 5-1 for a dark green. You can add some of the standard bright greens for a 'lift' and a touch of orange to add dirtiness if your green is too bright or black if the colour is too light. You may find it best to leave your inks to dry and concentrate a little if they are too thin.

The longer you leave a leaf in your inks when dip painting the stronger the colour, as the vellum or paper will absorb more ink. You can layer up by dipping, drying and dipping again.

See the first project, grasses.

Gerbera petals drying
Below: tree leaves

Simple flowers & leaves

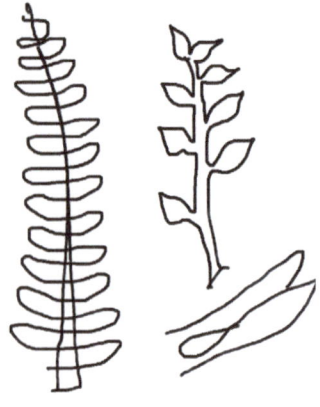

Filler plants & leaves... and planting them

Because flowers are time consuming to make, one of the easiest ways to fill out your scene is to make plenty of leaves and vines etc. which can be used as a background for more time consuming elements.

This also gives you time and space to get your head around lots of different greens.

Also some of these leaves and twiggy elements add height and drama to the display so it's worth having some of these made up in various shades.

Colour

Green is the most difficult colour to get right especially as you might be displaying your miniatures under a different light than the one you mixed your colour under. They may look totally different in these different settings. This is called metamerism.

Also when using inks the particles of colour can separate and flow off to the edges or appear to disappear altogether especially when drying on kitchen towels or blotting paper.

I found my early greens using Ecoline inks looked perfect when applied but became less bright and more brown when dry meaning I had to repaint a lot of my early work.

If you are interested in the subject of colour and metamerism and especially if you use polymer clay I have a book called Angie Scarr's Colour Book which might interest you.

Grasses can be simply dip dyed or you can take more time to paint them carefully.

If you want a deeper colour dip, dry and then dip again. Or dip and then paint over. This gives you time to check your colours and add a brighter green if your colour is too dull, or a darker green if your colour is too light.

Grasses can be made as a strip or fan. This way they can be simply rolled or folded to plant simply into a plant pot.

To fill your plant pot really simply put a small pebble or some sand etc. in the bottom of the pot. Add a little Oasis to the top and then press down a little so it's lower than the rim. Coat in PVA glue and scenic material or dried coconut husk etc. Poke holes in this with a cocktail stick and add more PVA glue. Fold or roll your grasses and press into these holes. Leave to dry.

Tree branch designs

I have some tree branch designs in my sets too. These need a bit of reinforcement by adding wires, or paper cord. If you are using a fine nozzle glue bottle you can feed the wire or cord into the nozzle. Squeeze the bottle a bit and pull it out. It should come out coated in glue and ready to attach to the branches.

Twigs

For a more opaque look use paper. You can use a thicker vellum for strength and this can mean that you may not need to wire these elements in a floral bouquet.

We designed these elements to be as snag free as possible but due to their tiny size and complexity any problems with glue on a blade or bluntness or poor adhesion to your mat will result in some pieces snagging.

These elements are designed to give extra drama to floral displays and bouquets so you can go crazy colour wise with these. Paint brown for standard twiggy elements, but try painting white and adding glitter, or silver or gold. You can also use these to support leaves and flowers.

Tropical palm, fern and ZZ plant

I used paper covered floral wire and fast setting PVA glue to wire the stems of the palm and ZZ plant.

Fern

For the fern plants I use paper cord for the stems. The ends can then be curled to create the fiddlehead effect if you wish. The curl goes forwards,

Vines

These are really useful for adding a hanging element to your displays.

Some parts are very delicate in 12th scale. Make sure you adhere well but not on too strong a grip. Remove from the mat carefully.

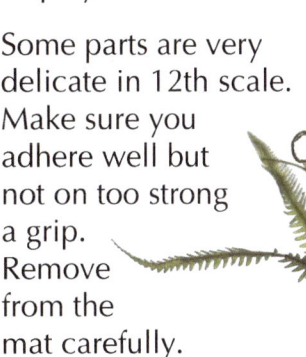

Suggested colouring, and uses for vines and bines

They can be coloured with alcohol inks, paints or Sharpie type pens. Some curling will happen naturally when painting but can also be shaped using a ball tool on a foam mat. Try variegated ivy.

With the grape vines try fresher green on smaller leaves. Or try putting a touch of ochre on the tips.

Try fresh green on the hops… or a brownish ochre for dried hops. Try drawing in veins with a sharpened wax pencil which will resist the ink.

Try adding to branches (dried herb roots shown in the photo on page 8) or miniature trees fences, pergolas. Try twining more than one together or glueing end to end. Put 'dried' hops over a bar in a pub scene. Wrap into miniature wreaths, to use as decorations for Xmas scenes. Can be used as table decorations, additions to gift envelopes place markers greetings cards etc.

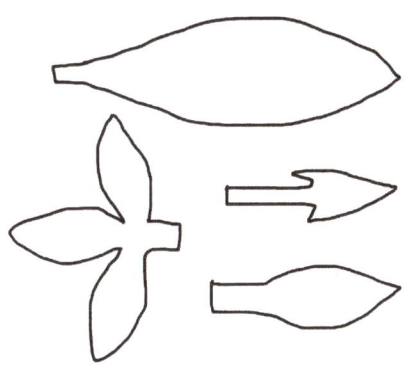

Bird of Paradise

You will need
Size 24 or 26 flower wire for this project

Although these flowers look really unusual they are the easiest of all to make!

Paint the petals a really vibrant orange. The little arrow shapes in bright indigo blue. You can tip the edges of these with a little orange.

You might also wish to colour the tip of a leaf part. Take a look at a photograph of a bird of paradise flower.

To assemble
Fold the 3 petal part, so that one petal sits between the other 2. You need 2 or 3 sets for each complete flower. Glue on the end of a piece of flower wire using fast grab glue. Add one blue arrow shape to each petal set.

Then take a medium size leaf part and wrap around the top, covering the base of the petal parts. Bend the stem if you haven't already.

Then add a really small leaf part on the place where the stem starts to bend. This will stand upright in the same direction as the main stem.

I double paint the large leaves. I dip-paint them lightly once before folding. Then I fold them very sharply. I repaint the edges of the leaf using the curling effect of the water in the ink to give the leaves some shape. In the case of the ones which enfold the flower you may wish to add other colours subtly to the edge.

I add one leaf to each flower stem but how you use the larger leaves (if at all) is up to you.

You could plant flowers in a clay pot filled with Oasis foam covered in glue and scenic material, of course you can also put them in vases, flower arrangements or exotic window boxes. See our files for window boxes.

Sunflower

You will need
Size 22 or 24 flower wire for this project
Scenic scatter at least 2 colours in the brown, orange and green spectrums
Eva foam or similar

You can make the calyx simply by dipping a smaller petals in green.

Dip the rest in a really sunny yellow ink or paint.

For the leaves I chose to draw veins with a fountain pen and wash with a mix of green ecoline inks.

To assemble

Cut your wire to around 8 cm lengths. Cut one end on an angle so that the end of the wire will pierce the paper/vellum.

With a pair of small needle nose pliers, wrap the blunt end of the wire round the pliers to make a circle of 3-5mm across, then continue to wind so that the next bit of wire goes inside this circle forming a bit of inner concentric circle then pull the wire downwards and inwards so that it stands in the middle of the circle and at 90 degrees.

This idea will form the basis of many (but not all) of your flower designs so do make sure that you get some practice on this bigger flower.

Use a piece of EVA foam as a base, with a large ball tool, roll around the middle of the calyx to cause it to indent a little

Using the end of the wire or your pointed tweezers stab through the paper or vellum in the middle and feed it up the stem until it sits just behind the loop. Add a generous blob of

glue before fully bringing the calyx up to the wire.

Indent the middle of the petals then turn each one and roll round the underneath of the petals to cause them to curve backwards slightly. Glue 3 or 4 petal sets on top. Making sure the petals line up to fill the empty spaces between the petals on the previous set.

You might wish to let the glue dry between layers. Add a fairly deep ring of glue round the edge of the central circle and turn upside down and dip into scenic materials. You can choose the colour from brown through orange to green(It depends how mature the seeds are).

Leave this covered ring to dry before adding a thinner layer of glue to the centre circle and adding another colour of scenic materials to this centre, shaking any excess off.

Add the leaves by applying glue all the way down the stem part of the leaf and sticking it onto the flower wire wrapping it round the wire and holding it in place with your fingers or several clips.

Finally bend the head of the flower over just a few millimetres behind the calyx to your desired position. Generally the flowers with the more mature (brownish) seeds will bend over furthest. 'Younger' flowers may stand straight up and their petals may not curve backwards. You can choose to cut even smaller sunflowers but be aware that their petals are weaker at a smaller size and you might wish to cut larger Gerbera for this instead.

Gerbera, ox eye daisy and echinacea

You will need

Size 24 or 26 flower wire for this project
Scenic scatter various colours

Optional:
Eva foam or similar
Oasis flower foam or similar

Although gerbera are a nice simple flower to make from the parts and are my absolute favourites, at 12th scale we are working at the very limits of what the cutters can do since there are lots of tight little turns.

We had to reduce the number of petals to 8 and increase the number of layers we recommended in order to get a good result.

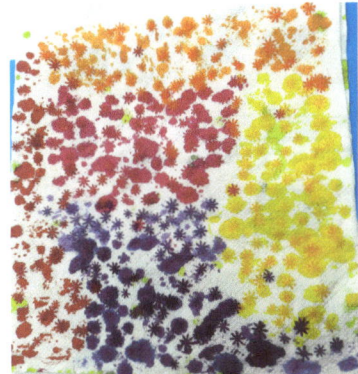

Gerberas come in many delightful colours. My advice is simply to Google images for gerbera colours.

You can also make a calyx simply by dipping some of the smaller petals in green.

To assemble

Cut your wire to around 4 cm lengths cutting on an angle so that the end of the wire will pierce the paper/vellum

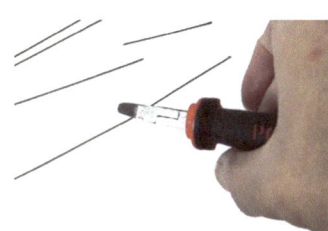

Stab the wire right through the green calyx and then bend the very tip over to 90 degrees. Add glue to the centre of this bend. Push the calyx up to it and and press the first petal on to it.

Put this into Oasis dry flower foam to dry while you carry on making more flowers.

I like to cut my Oasis into triangles as you can get more flowers into a triangle and it's a very stable shape.

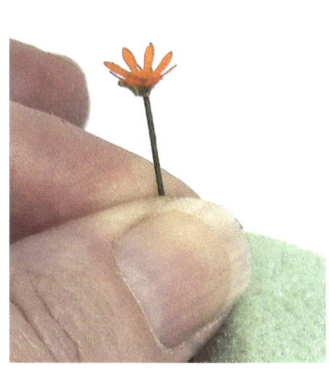

Use an EVA foam pad to press a large ball tool into the centre of the second and subsequent layers.

You can also use the ball around the edges on the other side if you want them to curl backwards a bit. Dry between each layer of petals.

You need to use a minimum of 3 layers but 4 or 5 is better depending on how thick your paper/vellum is. Start with larger petal pieces and on subsequent layers you can go smaller. Make sure that your second layer of petals fill in the empty spaces left by the first layer. Continue filling in with smaller petal pieces.

Put a little blob of glue in the middle of the flower and dip into flock or scenic material or flower soft. You can use the flat back of a cocktail stick or a ball tool to press the middle a little. This reshapes it into a pleasing and realistic flower centre. Some gerbera have a darker coloured centre.

You can pop extra glue in and add a second colour to this when the first layer is dry.

Do not flatten the blob of glue and scenic material on the echinacea. Leave to dry into a raised 'blob'. In the case of the ox eye daisy you can touch lightly to flatten when it is half dry. I select the largest size petals for echinacea and smaller ones for daisies.

For ox eye daisy and echinacea select a thinner flower wire (30 is good) bend the top of the wire into the smallest possible circle on the end of your tweezers and bend that circle over so it sits like a flat halo above the stem glue a blob of glue to the end of the wire and dipinto scenic material. Then 'thread' the petal pieces on from the bottom.

Summer Flowers

Wildflowers

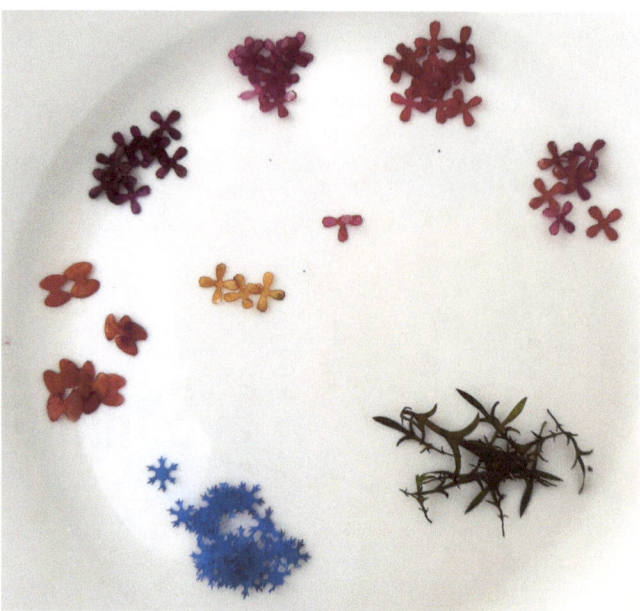

Now we're getting on to more difficult flowers. We really are making the machine work for its money on the cornflowers.

These flowers are very delicate so If you find that they do not cut well with your machine size the flowers up by 20% and try again, or replace your blade or change your mat or material.

Use fine flower wire and a very fine pair of tweezers (beading tweezers). Twist the top of the flower wire round the end of the tweezers and bend to 90 degrees. Pull out the tweezer end and arrange the loop over the top of the wire stem.

Remember to cut the wire at an angle so you can push through the centre of the petals, 2 petals per flower. You might need to pierce the petal piece first if using vellum. I use the tip of my finest tweezers on EVA foam. Glue behind the petals using a fine tipped glue bottle and fast grab rapid set glue. Finally, glue the centre with a small blob and dip in purple flock for the cornflowers, black flock for the poppies and yellow flock for the cosmos. Cosmos come in many colours so have fun!

Add the leaves to the stems by glueing light lines on the stem where you want the leaf to sit if they are going to be presented as growing flowers.

Dahlia

Large scale cuts

Put your first petal on the wire and make a loop pressed down at 90 degrees to stop the petal slipping off. Or you can thread a very tiny seed bead on to the wire before adding the petals smallest first.

Glue the first petal parts and hold for a minute or two right round the bead while the glue dries.

Then add extra petals getting larger as you go until you have a really packed little flower with the last of the petals and the calyx folding backwards.

Fold a leaf in half and attach to the stem along the bottom half of the centre crease. You may need clips to hold this on until it dries.

Carnation and African marigold

In my examples I cut in vellum for the lovely delicate translucency. Use either a light grip or standard grip cutting mat. I coloured in Ecoline artists inks before removing them from the cutting mat. Remove carefully as folds can cause tears in vellum. Painting before removing from the mat makes a lovely outlined effect and also helps you to 'weed' the tiny flowers and leaves from the rest of the paper. You can draw pink lines on the carnations before flooding with colour if you want that subtle effect. Draw lines before removing from the

mat That makes it easiest to get the marks on every one without having to hold them! If you prefer to paint after removing from the mat dip both sides or paint both sides so that the paper doesn't curl too dramatically.

if it doesn't stay on the first time! You can stand these up in flower foam.

For the flowers
Make a small hole in the centre of each petal by pushing a sewing needle or the tip of your tweezers into it. This is easiest on EVA foam.

Wind the very tip of a piece of wire to form a very small loop. Select one of the smaller petals and push the tip of the wire through the hole threading the petal onto and right up the wire.

Leaves
Take a 2 inch (5cm) approx piece of wire and push it into the tip of your glue bottle. Squeeze the bottle slightly drawing the wire back out at the same time. This will coat the wire evenly.

Press the wire gently to the back of a leaf part. This takes some practise so don't get frustrated

Put a tiny dot of glue on to the loop in the wire and pinch the first petal in at the top to cover the wire completely. Thread another small petal on adding glue just under the last petal. Thread on a slightly larger size petal and continue until you are happy with your flower shape and density.

Put a tiny blob of glue behind the petals to simulate the deep calyx that a carnation has and paint this and the wire later when it is dry. Make sure you use paint for this and not the inks as they won't dry on wire or glue. You can make flower buds in a similar way. If you want a little more curve to your petals you can use a ball tool on an EVA foam mat as you did with the roses.

Roses

Start with the central petal part. This is the curved strip. (The wild rose doesn't have this centre.) Using the foam to press into, run the ball tool round the inner edge of each petal in the strip so that it curls up a little at the end.

There are 4 styles of rose in our bundle. A simple petalled rose, a heart shape petal, a Campanella (frilly edged rose) and a small wild rose.

The wild rose needs some kind of filament. I use a short bundle of yellow thread passed through the loop which you make in the wire, and glued on with fast grab glue. You can put filaments in all types but I generally don't bother with the larger roses as the petals are so tightly packed, I don't need them.

Do the same to the sets of 3, then flip them and press the ball tool into the base of each petal (you do not need to do this to the strip).

Using a cocktail stick wrap the petal strip round and round the end of the cocktail stick with the straight edge at the tip. Start with the smallest petal end.

Take a piece of flower wire the length you want the stem, plus a few millimetres (or you can use any craft wire).

Using wire cutters, cut diagonally so that one end is sharp.

Using pointed tweezers make a very small loop in the other (non sharp) end of the wire.

Bend the circle over at 90 degrees to the stem and adjust so that it will lie flat within the centre of the flower.

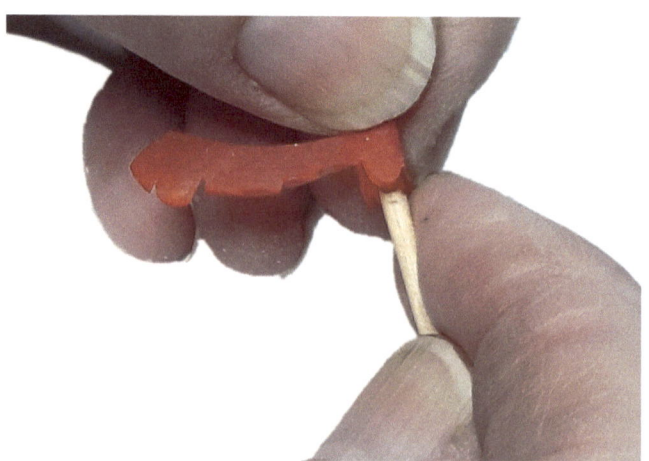

Grip the full set of petals and slide it off the cocktail stick. Keep it in the short cylinder shape while you apply glue liberally to the end.

Glue the middle petals to the centre of one of the smaller shaped petal pieces. Then glue onto another set with the petals spun to be between the first set. You can add as many extra petals as you want and you can draw them up round the central petals for a smaller rose or leave them wider open for a more open bloom.

Add the calyx by piercing the centre with your tweezers push the end of the stem through and draw the calyx up to the underneath of the loop. Then you can glue the flower to the loop and the calyx.

You can hold it until the glue starts to dry or you can use a craft clothes peg or clip to hold it together until the glue partly dries and fully 'grabs'.

You can now add the optional leaf part a little way down the stem using glue on the stem. Leave the top leaf unglued (you can also shape the leaves a little before adding them).

Finally add a leaf set to the stem leaving at least one leaf free from the stem. You can pre wire the leaves if you want to arrange them or to make into a rose bush.

Freesias

A blunted cocktail stick is useful for this project

These next two flowers come in long stems of blooms. Each one has its own individual calyx and I'm lazy, so I didn't want to make each flower individually and attach it to the flower. I lie awake first thing in the morning trying to solve this kind of problem. I'm strange like that! So the fixes I came up with are nice and simple. I put the calyxes as simple wrap rounds. Or rather a wrap up for the freesia and round for the gladioli.

For the freesia, I put two stems back to back to make them easier to cut and so that the pairs, when they line up, hold each flower.

Using very fine flower wire, glue 2 calyx/stem pieces back to back on the end of a piece of wire making sure that the calyx pieces fall opposite each other so that they fill in the gaps between the ones on the other side. This is a fiddly little job if you aren't dextrous but if you are patient the first time, or at least swear a little but ry again, it will soon come easily to you.

When dry, fold these together to one side leaving just enough gap to get the flowers between them.

Using a medium to small ball tool, press each petal on a piece of EVA foam, to re-shape it into an inward curl. The smaller your ball tool the tighter your shape will be. Put 2 parts together using a blob of glue in the middle and make sure the second layer in-fills the gaps in the first.

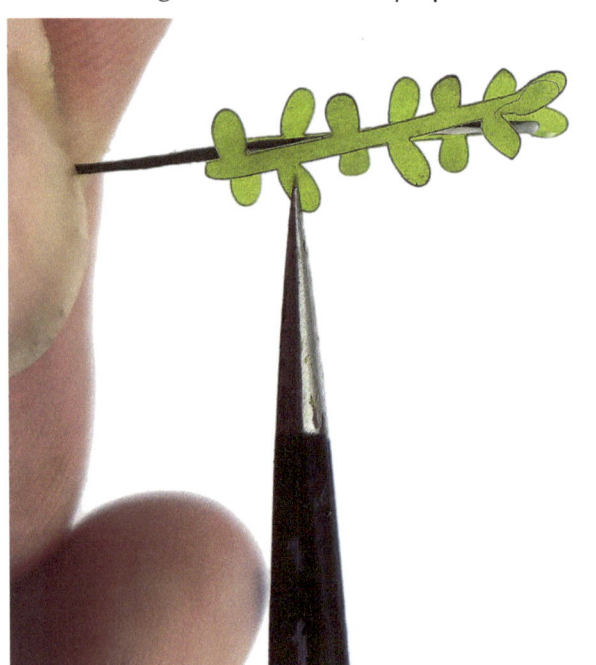

Use a blunted cocktail stick, to push into the centre to reshape the flowers. If you want an OPEN flower turn it upside down and as you push into the middle the petals will come up open. If you want a closed flower (most freesias are closed) press inside the petals and they will curl inwards. Once you have pressed them you can make the flower tighter and longer by squeezing the base of it between your fingers.

Bend the end of the calyx stem over into a hockey stick shape so that the calyxes are sticking up

Put a drop of glue between the bottom pair of calyxes and press one of the largest flowers into it. Use the cocktail stick. A tiny touch of glue on the stick will help you to pick it up and place it.

Use a little twist to remove the stick while holding the flower into the calyx.

Move to smaller and smaller flowers as you go towards the tip. I use a single set of petals towards the end and then sometimes tear off one petal and twist it into a tight little tube to make the last one so it's almost invisible.

You can add a leaf to the stem or 'plant' them separately, either wired or unwired. Folding the leaves slightly gives them more strength if you want a straighter, more rigid leaf.

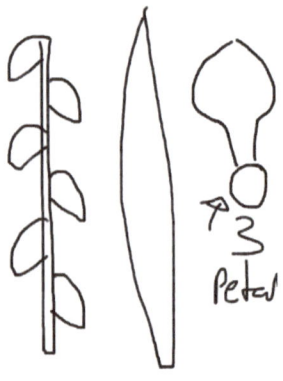

Gladioli

I dip paint the leaves once and then make a sharp, creased fold. Then I open it out and repaint it with a brush.

Glue the long calyx piece (after painting and drying) to a flower wire. Leave to dry.

Then curl each of the little quarter circles into a cone shape. You get hold of the bottom with the tiny tweezers and curl them round into a cone shape, glue and hold it for a moment Then you go to the next one.

I find it easiest to do all of the 'cones' on one side first. Then move on to the other side. It may take a little practice but you can get quite quick at this.

You need to be a little bit more gentle with the top ones.

Next thing you need to do is to make sure that these stay in place so in each case you need to put a little line of glue on the side of each of these little curls. You may need to hold them in place until the glue grabs in some cases.

Next you need to press the petals with a ball tool to help them to curl. Start with the bigger petals. (you've got three sizes of petals). You need 2 petals for each flower so that's a lot of petals in each stem!

When they are pressed to curve, in this case, they are actually upside down, so we need to turn them over. Start with the largest petal pieces.

Put a spot of glue in the middle of one of them and just a little spot of glue on your cocktail stick to help you pick up a second petal piece. Place the second piece over the first one so that the petals go between the ones on the first set. Press the middle so they glue together and shape into a flower with a lower centre. You might want to manipulate this shape with your fingers to enhance the 'trumpet' shape.

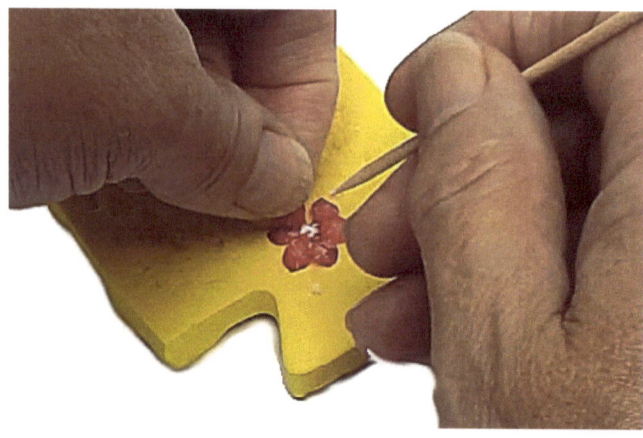

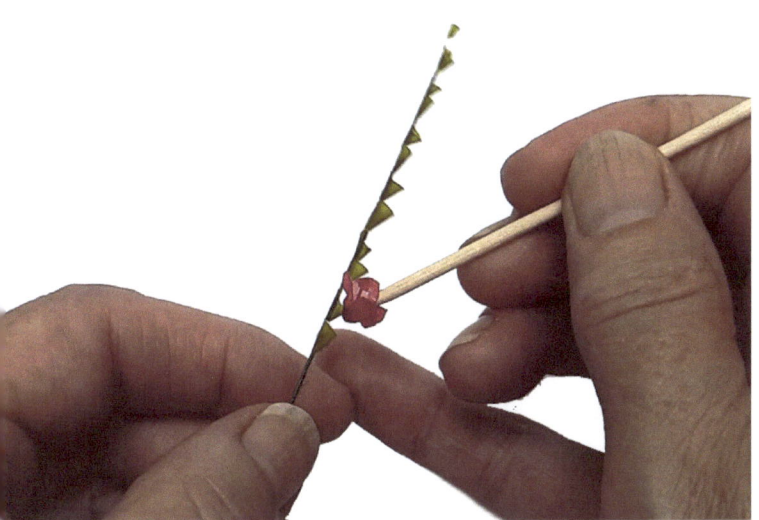

So now this flower goes into one of these little cone shapes. Put some glue into the bottom cone and then press the flower with the stick.

Twist the cocktail stick as you pull it out. If you don't twist, it often brings the flower out as well. Hold for a few moments so that the glue grabs well. You can carry on holding this part while working on the next flowers. Repeat with big flowers until you get about half way up the length when you can switch to the medium and then small flowers. You can do some inward facing like the freesias. Finally tear a single petal and roll it into a point and put that in one of the upper cones. Leave the last two or three cones empty or you can add extra small pointy petals.

There is a short video of this on YouTube at:

https://youtu.be/2NUw8Ex--wI

Xmas flowers and plants

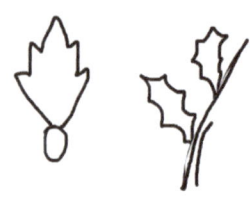
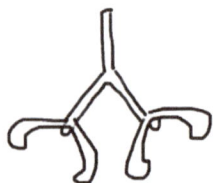

Hellebore

The hellebore, also known as Xmas rose, is a very delicate greenish white. There are some pink speckled and pink to deep burgundy coloured varieties too. Paint or dip in a thin opaque white paint with a very tiny touch of green added. You can add a little extra wash of green to the centre. If the original paint is not fully dry it should spread in a pleasing way.

The centre can be made with yellow scenic material. Simply pot a very small blob of glue and dip in yellow scenic material OR You can snip a small bundle of threads and glue on. Leave to dry before snipping shorter.

Holly

I put the leaves together on a stem in our design. This saves lots and lots of fiddly work.

Often because of how very complex this cut is, and because I cut on vellum which is tougher than paper, the branches often cling to the paper backing. This means I can remove the whole sheet and do the colouring off the mat but on the sheet.

Because of this I can colour the stems differently. So because orange and green together make brown I colour the stems orange first on both sides of the vellum, then I overlay with green several times increasing the intensity of the green just on the leaves. Then I have to remove the stems really delicately. Of course I lose a few leaves. But I can always add more since I also cut some doubles and triples as extras to apply later to give extra 3 dimensionality.

You can choose to wire this or to wrap it round dried roots. I dry roots from my basil plants as they dry well and smell nice. They also make lovely 12th scale branches and twigs.

Add blobs of red glue or red tiny)1mm) red no hole beads. It can be quite difficult to find exactlñy the right red for holly berries. Mine were a little translucent. You can paint after gluing but that does often shop up as splodges so if you can find the right colour beads, so much the better.

Mistletoe

Use a light or medium tack cutting board (in very good condition), roller really well on to the surface to make sure you have excellent adhesion, remove waste paper and leaves carefully as some elements are delicate.

After painting add a blob of glue to the centre dot between the leaves

You can get a pearl powder that has a green sheen that looks lovely mixed with the glue for this job. Or you can simply use a pearl coloured 2mm no-hole bead.

Poinsettia

I will call these petals even though they are all leaf bracts. The large size are in green. The very small and the medium size are in red. You choose the complimentary darker colours for the veins. I use dark burgundy.

I use yellow or very light green beads on the top petal.

When finished, assemble using a wire approximately 2 inches (5 cm) long with a loop bent on the end. The other end should be cut at an angle so it is really sharp. Glue one of the petal pieces face up (with the little blobs upwards) on the top of the loop. Then put another blob of glue behind the petal and add another petal.

Add another blob of glue and thread another small petal on. Take care when piercing the petal part to avoid pricking your fingers on the wire. I use a piece of expanded foam for this.

Add another slightly larger petal and continue adding a bead then a blob of glue and a petal. You can decide how many of each size you use and whether to plant one or more of these plants in a plant pot vase or table decoration etc.

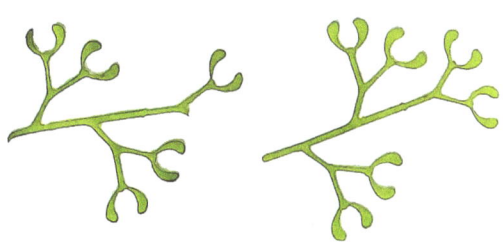
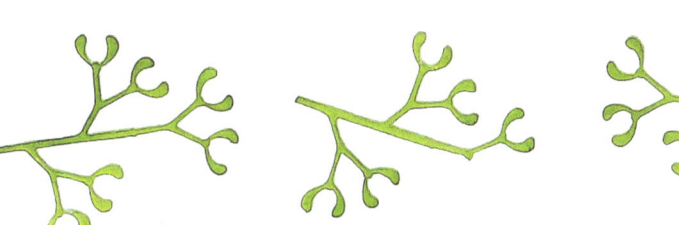

Spring flowers

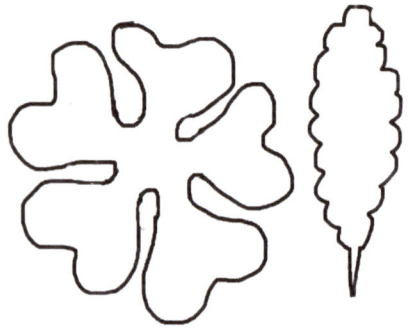

Primroses and violets

I use very fine beading wire and fast setting PVA glue. The 'soil' in the polymer clay pots is made with Oasis dry flower foam painted with a mix of PVA glue and brown scenic material.

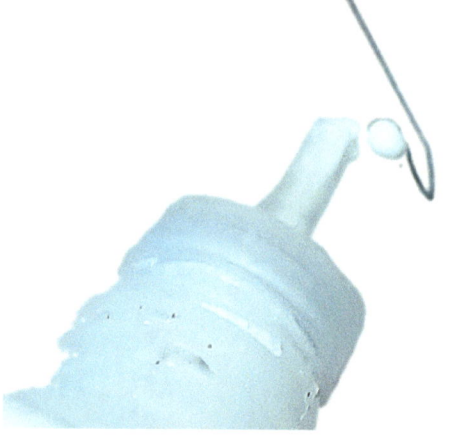

Press the centres of your flowers with a blunt cocktail stick or tweezers so that the petals 'lift'. You can spend extra time shaping the petals if you wish.

Form a loop in the end of some very fine flower or beading wire (I have used very fine beading wire)

Bend the loop to face forwards (at 90 degrees to the wire). Put a small blob of PVA glue on the loop and press the flower on to the glue.

(Shown is the wire for violets, already bent. Leave straight for primroses.)

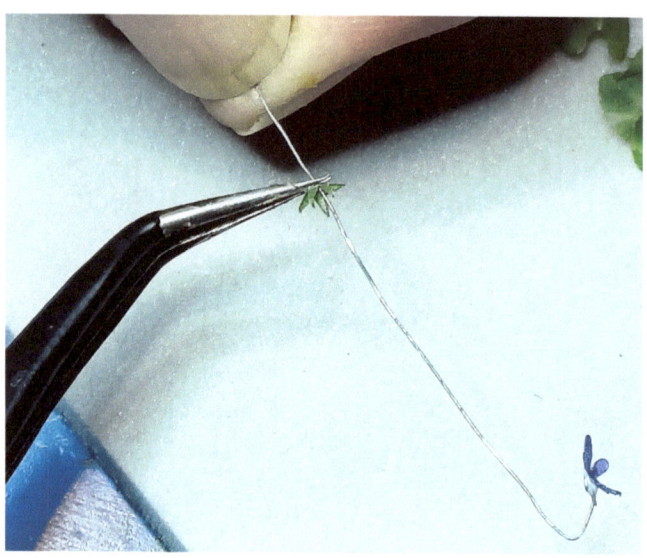

Violets

Bend the wire into a shepherds crook shaped bend so that the flower points slightly upwards but then the stem curves down for a millimetre

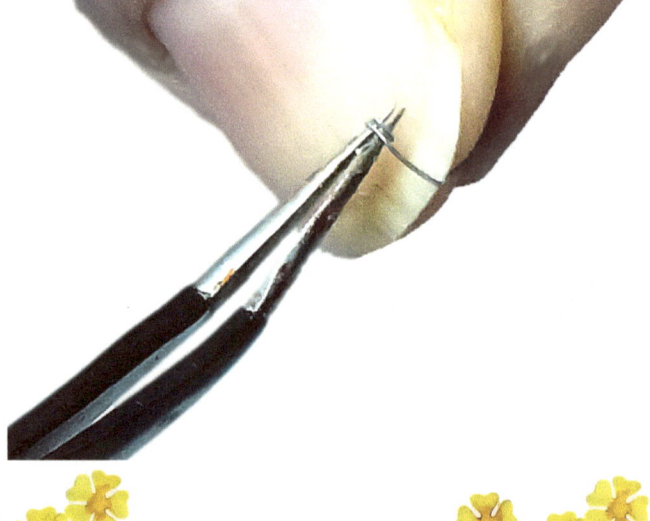

and up again for several millimetres before turning down again. If you are unsure of this shape look at wild violet photographs on Google. Press the flower pieces into shape and glue to the loop.

Put a hole into the star shaped calyx with the end of your tweezers or with a sewing needle or pin. Feed the star onto the bottom of the wire and pass all the way up to the flower back.

Put a spot of glue behind the flower before attaching the calyx.

Leaves
Put glue on to a piece of wire and press to the back of the leaf (not shown). I feed the wire into the top of the glue bottle and squeeze and then draw it out. This leaves the wire well coated in glue.

Primrose
Colour the petals in pale yellow. Add a ring of orange with a felt-tip pen. You could also add a dot of green in the very centre. Wire the leaves individually.

The colours of yellow primroses and purple violets look particularly pleasing together, and happen to be out at the same time of year.

Daffodils

Prepare your stems by holding some very fine flower wire between your tweezers close to, but not at the tip. Wind the wire round the tip of the tweezers approx 4 times so that the wire forms a tiny cone. Leave the rest of the wire

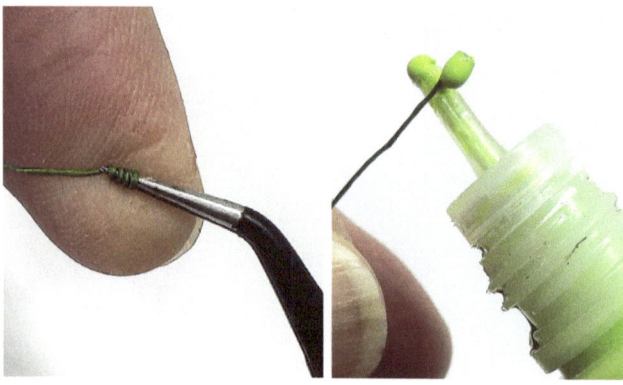

sticking out at 90 degrees.

Put a small blob of green PVA glue on the end of the cone. Leave to dry.

Take a 'trumpet' piece (the long 'frilly' bit). Bend the little frilled edge outwards. I have designed two depths of trumpet piece. I use

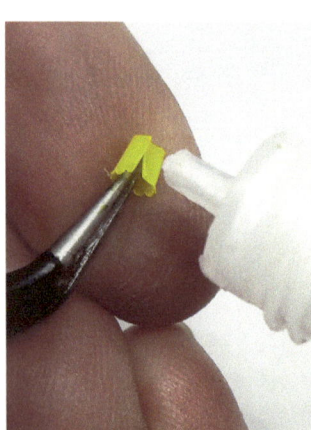

the narrower one for the orange edged narcissus flower and the wider one for the classic all yellow daffodil. Form the slightly trumpet shaped conical flower centre and glue the tab.

You can choose the size of your trumpet by adjusting the crossover. Hold the join together for a few moments with your tweezers until it sticks. Glue one set of 3 petals to another to form the classic daffodil star shape.

Put glue on the bottom edge of the trumpet and add to the flower centre.

Leave to dry.

Press the entire flower onto a blob glue on the end of your prepared wire cone.

Leave to dry. You can bend the heads over when the glue has dried.

Crocus

Note crocus are much shorter than daffodils: around one third as tall.

Form a very small loop in the end of some very fine flower wire (to stop the wire sliding right through the paper).

Put a hole into the smaller petal set with the

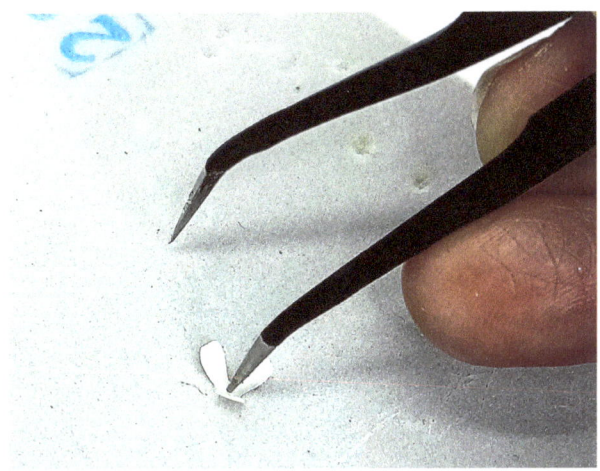

end of your tweezers or with a sewing needle or pin.

Put a spot of glue on the loop.

Feed the petal onto the bottom of the wire and pass all the way up to the loop.

Hold the petals together until the glue grabs. A couple of minutes should do.

Then pierce and add the larger petal set. You can add curvature with a ball tool if you wish.

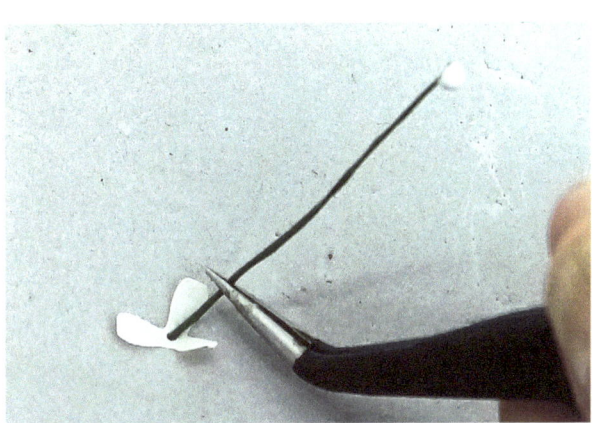

Put a spot of glue behind the flower before attaching the second petal. Arrange so the petals fill in between the first set.

Add the single leaf to the stem of the flower allowing a little of the leaf to come up the side of the flower. The length of the leaf indicates the approximate length of the stem.

Leaves

The leaves in this set do not need wiring, but the extra crocus leaves should be wound round the end of the tweezers to form a 'bundle'. You can halve the set to form smaller bundles.

I have 'planted' my flowers in Oasis foam covered in glue and scenic material to form a flower bed, of course you can also put them in pots.

5 + 6 Petals

Cyclamen

I used vellum for the flowers and leaves and coloured with Ecoline inks and some with white acrylic paint. You can colour with your favourite paints.

I also used a masking pen (optional) to cover the areas of vellum I didn't want to paint. You can simply pick out in another colour/shade to get the detail.

You will also need size 30 or 32 paper coated flower wire.

Make a very small loop in the end of some flower wire using jeweller tweezers. Turn the loop to 90 degrees so that it lays flat across the top of the stem.

Add a blob of glue to the top of the loop and press the flower petals on ensuring the loop is fully covered by the centre of the petals. If it doesn't cover the loop your loop is too large. Leave the flowers to dry. When the glue dries you can turn the flower petals back towards the stem. Then form a hook shape at the flower end.

The leaves can also be wired in advance by sticking flower wire to the backs of the leaves.

I apply the glue by feeding the wire into the bottle tip and squeezing to apply the glue.

When you pull the wire out it should be evenly coated with glue. Leave to dry before bending the leaves at approx 90 degrees.

My pot in this case is filled with polymer clay and scenic scatter and drilled before glueing the plants in. You could use Oasis flower foam covered in scenic scatter as long as your pot is heavy enough.

Bluebells and Snowdrops

These are really stupidly tiny and are not for the faint hearted!

They are for this reason a bit big for 12th scale to make them easier to handle. Confident makers can adjust the size down around 10-15%.

Bluebells

Glue one set of 3 petals to another to form tiny star shapes press the middle of this star. Leave to dry. When dry

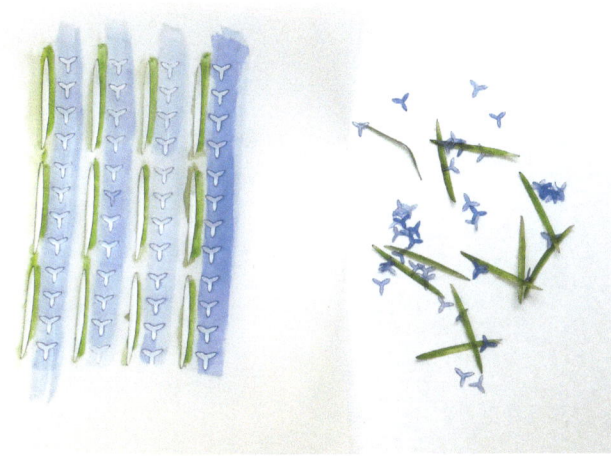

press each star firmly with a blunt edged craft tool or a blunted cocktail stick.

Hold some very fine flower wire between your tweezers bend the wire. Put a small blob of PVA glue on the end of the wire and attach a 'bell'.

Add 2 or three dots down one side of the wire a few millimetres apart and press on 2 more bells facing a little downwards. When these have 'grabbed' put 2 or three dots on the other side and add more bells.

Place the stem in Oasis foam to dry

Snowdrops

Form a very small loop (in exactly the same way as above) in the end of some very fine beading wire or the finest possible flower wire (to stop the wire sliding right through the paper).

Pot a spot of glue on the loop.

Put a hole into the smaller petal set with the end of your tweezers or with a sewing needle or pin. Feed the petal onto the bottom of the wire and pass all the way up to the loop. Hold the petals together until the glue grabs. A couple of minutes should do. Then pierce and add the larger slimmer petal set. You can add

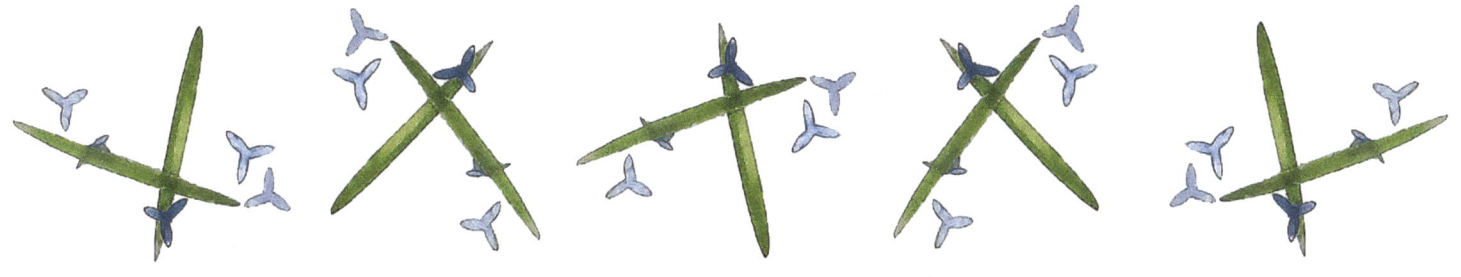

curvature with a ball tool if you wish. Put a spot of glue behind the flower before attaching the second petal arrange so the petals fill in between the first set. Add a blob more glue behind the second set of petals. If you have green glue use this. Leave the petals standing upright until the glue dries completely then you can curve their little heads over. You can choose to attach one of the leaves to the stem with glue or you can simply paint or draw on to the wire to make it green.

Leaves

The leaves in this set do not need wiring, but you can fold the leaves together to make them stand more upright.

The pair of leaves is for the snowdrops. The sets of 3 are for the bluebells.

I have 'planted' my flowers in a polymer clay pot filled with Oasis foam covered in glue and scenic material, of course you can also put them in vases.

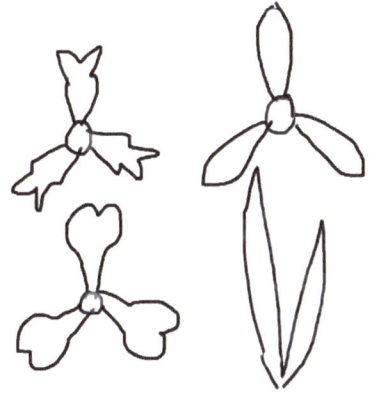

Iris

I coloured in Ecoline artists inks, I used an eye dropper to put in the yellow, and used an extremely fine tipped paintbrush for the lines, before removing from the cutting mat. If I were to do it again I'd use fountain pens.

 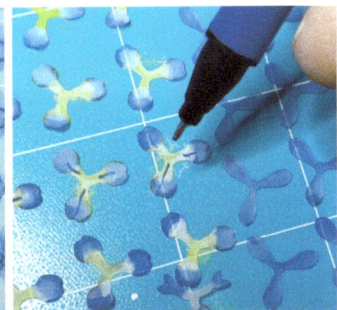

There are 3 types of petals. The rounded end ones are the central petals. The narrow divided ones are the second layer and the slightly divided curved ones are the bottom layer.

To assemble

Bend a loop into the end of a piece of wire.

Pierce the middle of the central petals, thread on to the other end of the wire and push up. Put glue on the loop and hold the petals together until the glue 'grabs'. You can curve the petal tips using your tweezers if you wish.

Take the slim second layer petal. Pierce that and thread the second layer up adding glue just before the petals meet.

Repeat with the outer petal.

Arrange the petals so that the bottom petals fall right down, unless you want them to look as if they are just opening.

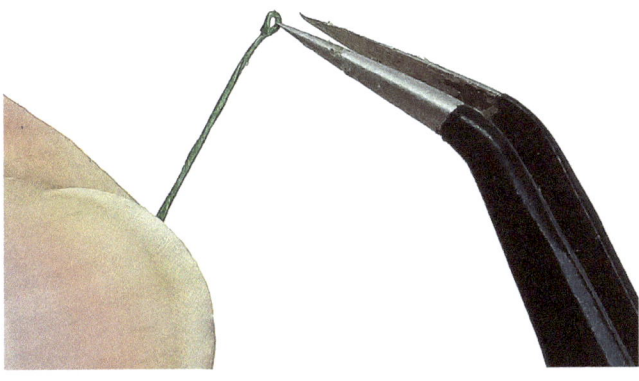 

Exotic and tropical plants

Swiss cheese plants (exotic 'holey' leaves)

Looking online for cheese plants (Monstera) throws up a whole range of exciting possibilities. I absolutely love the one that's more hole than leaf, so much that I bought a real one! This is where the cutter really comes into its own. When I make polymer clay plants using stencils this is one of the plants that stencilling wouldn't do because of the internal holes. There are ways but it's tricky and not as successful.

These simply need dip dying or painting but it's important to remember they don't want to be translucent they need to be opaque and the larger varieties are quite shiny. The smaller ones are less shiny. I use vellum for almost everything I make but in this case paper is possibly better. If using vellum make sure you paint well. You can paint the underside of the leaf a lighter green. If your paint does not have a sheen you will need to varnish them.

You can assemble larger plants by twisting the wires together and then coating with thick glue and paint to disguise the wire. Or you can use flower tape.

Acer bush

This is a particularly difficult and slow leaf for the machine to cut because there are lots and lots of changes of direction. When cutting just walk away for an hour! When we designed ours our software just hopped over all the 'teeth' on the leaves. Apparently this is a problem with using DXF files on the Silhouette machine. See problem solver.

I cut the leaves in vellum, you know that's my favourite by now! Of course it's a little more translucent than paper.

I painted with Ecoline inks. For more opacity you might wish to use acrylic paints. I use paper cord for the stems (you could use flower wire for a stiffer finish) Put the smaller leaves together in pairs at the end of the stems. Add extra larger leaves. Then glue the stems together. Finally glue extra leaves in the joins.

Plant using sharp tweezers and a little extra glue.

If you want to make 'the other plant that looks similar' you might wish to make a flower bud. You can find a nice scenic scatter and cut up some longer threads to give it extra texture and just place those on a blob of glue in between some smallish leaves on the tips of branches. I haven't done so here as this is a book for all. But this one is a very popular make.

Printing - prayer plants etc.

One of the brilliant things you can do with a cutter machine is line up prints and cuts, meaning you can get really complex leaf designs such as prayer plants and petal colourations. This is a little less 'artistic' in a sense but very effective. The one problem is that lining up can be tricky so you should make your print bigger so that any slight alignment issues don't affect the edges. You can even print both sides. Or print one side and paint the other. Prayer plants for example often have burgundy or purplish backs. Be aware that painting can make the paper wrinkle and be difficult to get fixed to the mat. Also print can peel off on the mat so it should be absolutely dry before attempting this and you might lose a mat because ink has peeled on to it. Perhaps better to paint the backs by hand. This also gives you the ability to touch up the edges as these can be obviously white otherwise.

We are only just getting to grips with this idea after Lisa (Sones-Peck) sent me an Ipad to try.

So this book doesn't prove the methods above that I intend to use, but they certainly could be your next step! Here I've worked out that if I use the rubber to draw white on a pre coloured leaf it's a lot easier!

Why do I draw my own leaves instead of just using photographs? Copyright. I absolutely respect copyright. All artists (and photographers) need to eat, and deserve income or at least kudos for their work and not to have it randomly used and abused. Also, it's simply more artistically satisfying to produce all of your work from scratch.

Alocasia amazonica

Orchids 3 styles

I cut the leaves and flowers in vellum, I painted with Ecoline inks and finished with Twinmarker colouring pens. For more opacity you might wish to use acrylic paints. I use paper cord (available at Angie Scarr Miniatures) for the stems (you could use flower wire for a stiffer finish) and fast setting PVA glue. The 'soil' can be made with Oasis dry flower foam painted with a mix of PVA glue and brown scenic material, or scenic scatter, glue and scenic material, or ground coconut husk etc.

The 'skinny' orchids just have one petal piece and the centre. The other two styles have the triple petals at the back overlaid with the double petal and the centre piece should be shaped slightly with a ball tool or a blunted cocktail stick. You can add a little dab of glue to the top of the centre piece. Add the first couple of leaf shapes to the stem to help give it stiffness for planting. Plant using sharp tweezers.

Since making these I bought some fountain pens with coloured inks and realised that they would be the very best way of painting the veins on orchids.

Display items for your scene

Plant pots, buckets and tall tubs or vases

Let's get started making some simple plant pots. When designing your own, refer to my instructions on making curves from parts of a circle. In our designs/bundle there are 5 sizes of plant pots.

First gently curve the main part and the trims (but not the base - star shape) card. To do this you put the dowel inside the card with your thumb on the side of the dowel and your finger under the card. Pull it across the card gently pressing on the back of the card with your finger/s. Repeat with the trims.

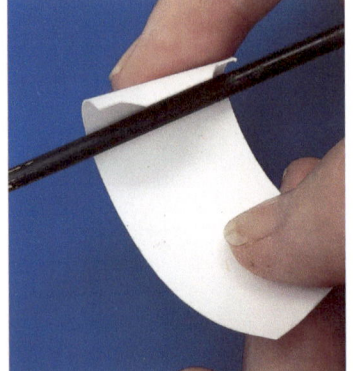
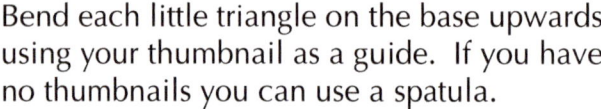

Add glue to the tab and carefully position making sure there is no crossover except the tab which should be inside the pot.

Bend each little triangle on the base upwards using your thumbnail as a guide. If you have no thumbnails you can use a spatula.

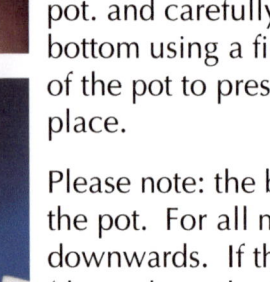

Put a line of glue inside the bottom of the pot. and carefully place the base into the bottom using a finger or dowel on the inside of the pot to press the triangular tabs into place.

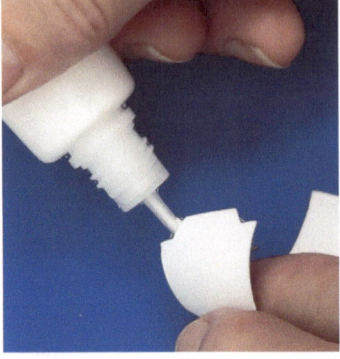

Please note: the base tabs go upwards inside the pot. For all my other planters they go downwards. If there are any slight gaps (depends on the thickness of your card and how you bend the tabs) you can fill with glue.

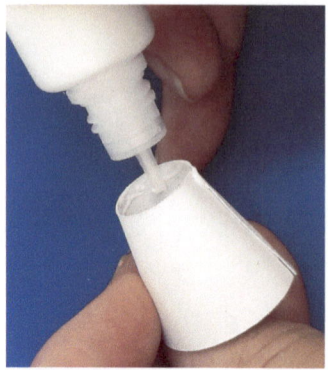

Add a thick line of glue to the outer edge of the top of the pot and add the trim. The longest edge at the top That is to say the 'bump' of the curve faces upwards. I set the edge a little away from the join in the main body for extra strength. Make sure the top of your trim exactly touches the edge of the pot.

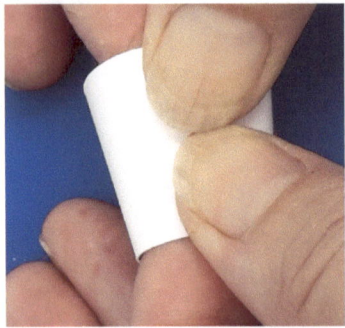
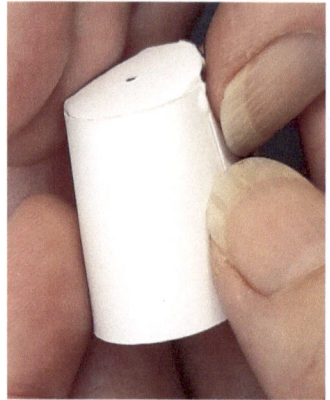

We have left the trim very slightly long to account for users of heavier card. Using the lighter card you will find you have a slight overlap (1-2mm). Snip this off carefully so that the card meets exactly.

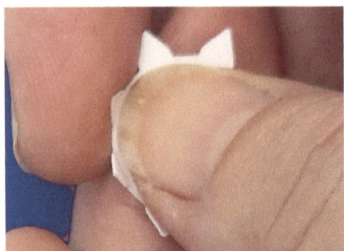
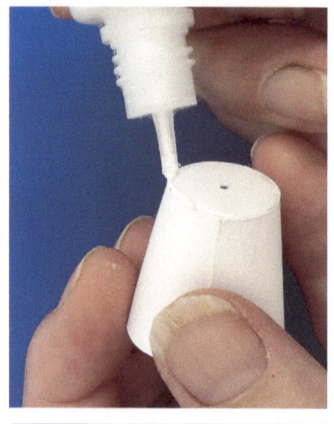

You can now add the optional second trim if you wish. If you want you can double the main trim and/or put more thin trims on for a slightly different effect.

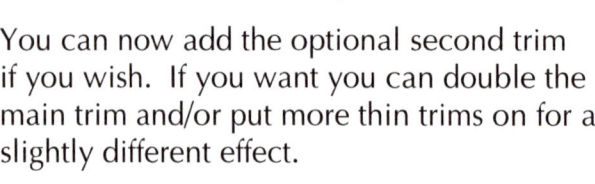
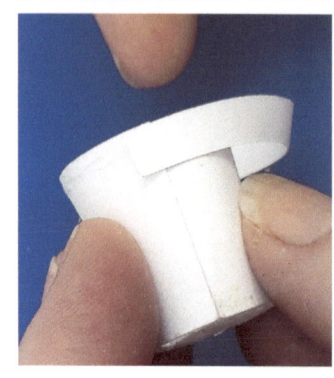

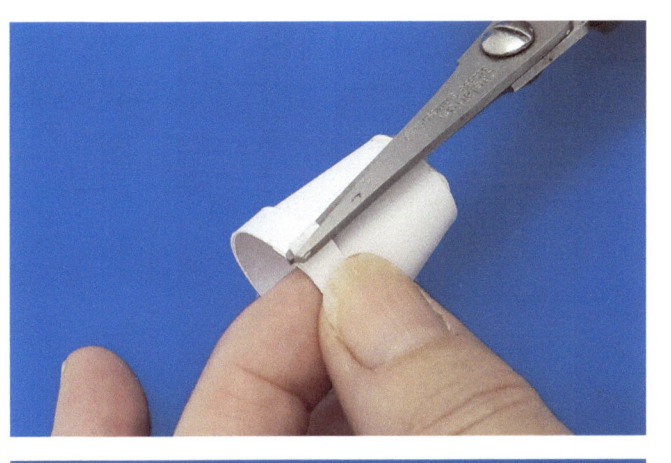
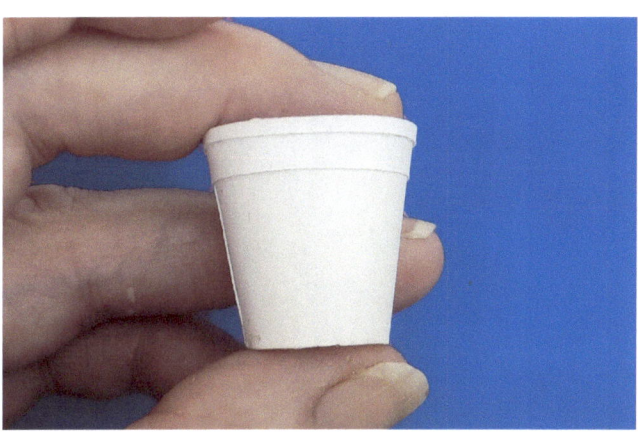
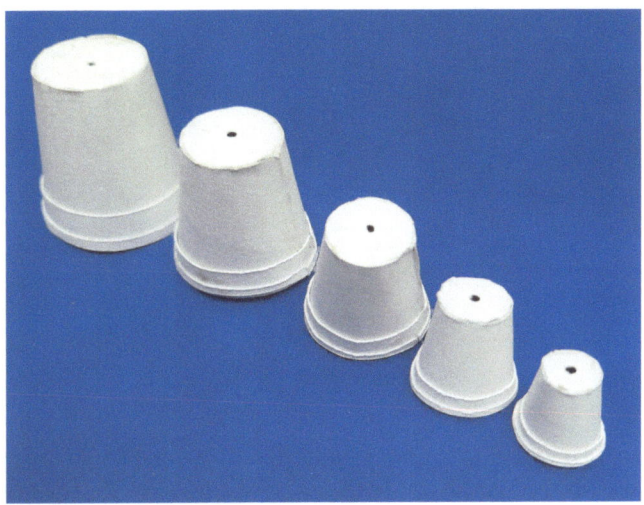

Plant pots can be filled with a weight at the bottom, Oasis to cover and then glue with scenic material for the soil on top.

If you are designing your own plant pots, buckets and jugs etc. It's worth remembering that all curves can be made using sections from circles. The size of the circle and what section you use determines the 'flare' on your item. So a small section from the outer edge of a BIG circle will have a very gentle flare, whereas a large section from a very small circle will have a very wide flare. In every case use fast grab/fast dry PVA glue and hold for a good few seconds until it sticks. In the case of these buckets etc, if you have curved them well there will be quite a lot of 'spring' in the card and you will need to hold them a bit longer or they will just spring open. The buckets and jugs look galvanised, when painted in matte silver paint or steel if in shiny silver. Of course you could also paint in pastel colours and hand paint the edges to look like enamelled buckets.

Explore your creativity. Your Cricut is a great tool for designing and making loads of lovely display items in card. We're just getting started. Look at the world around you for inspiration. I saw a tiny metal spiral staircase in an art shop in Greece. The same day I saw stairs covered in pots of flowers and I so wanted to put the two ideas together. If you are the kind who loves to design, there are no mistakes. After all, what have you got to lose? A few sheets of card and a few pleasant hours. If you aren't the designing type we have lots of these things for you. Just have fun with your paper and card miniature world!

Problem solver

Paper will not adhere to the mat

Your mat is old and has lost its stick. Certain papers and cards leave more particles on the surface. When working with miniature items the smallest lift or air bubble can leave you with a lot of frustration.

Your paper is slightly but not noticeably damp. This happens to us a lot as our machine is in an outside office as you can see, below.

Double cut

Your cutter may cut 2 lines instead of one. If you have a thick line in order to see the shape more easily, the machine can try to cut both sides of the line. If this happens, fill the shape in black, remove the line and the cutter will not try to cut twice.

It simply won't cut

There are times when you get no result, and the reasons can vary.

Check your blade. Is it sharp? One time the end was broken on one of ours and without looking closely there was no way to see what was wrong. With original blades quite expensive I didn't have many to swap out.

Is the blade depth set right? Again one of my expensive, original, blades had a habit of winding itself down to zero during a cut.

Have you actually got something to cut? Images and photos will not be cut, only line designs. If you need to cut it use the Trace option mentioned later.

Some machines allow more than two blades or tools, did you use the wrong one?

Sizing issues and fixes

Originally we added a 25.4mm / 1 inch green square to our designs as a reference so it could be easily scaled to size. This was convenient for flower designs but essential for structural elements. Cricut would bring each design in at a different scale and without it pieces wouldn't join up. Silhouette Studio was easy to set so that designs always came in at the specified size without extra effort, but Cricut Design

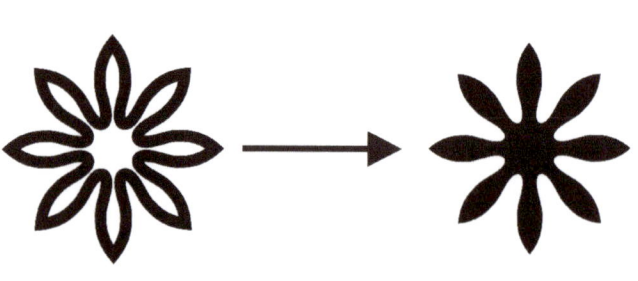

25.4mm / 1"

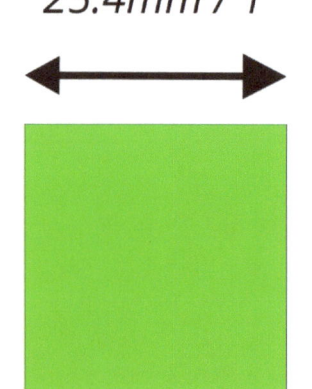

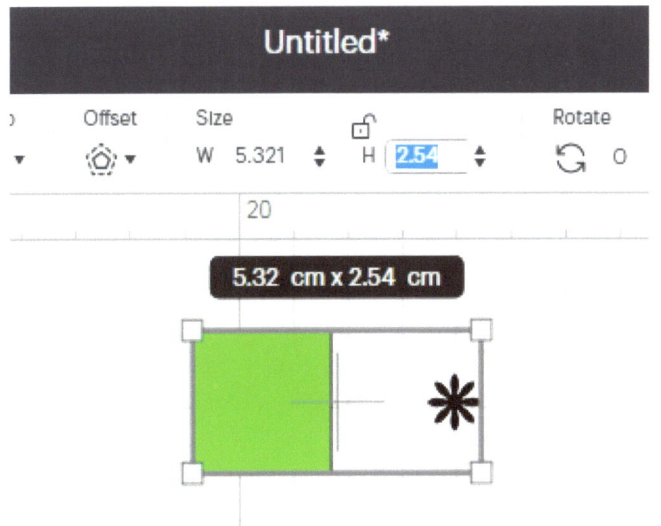

Space needed a work around. However at the time of writing Cricut stopped the work around with the green square. Now we have to specify the exact size of the design in centimetres and inches to apply it manually on a design by design basis.

Fold lines and perforations missing
Our structural designs often have fold lines, holes etc. on them to make assembly easier.

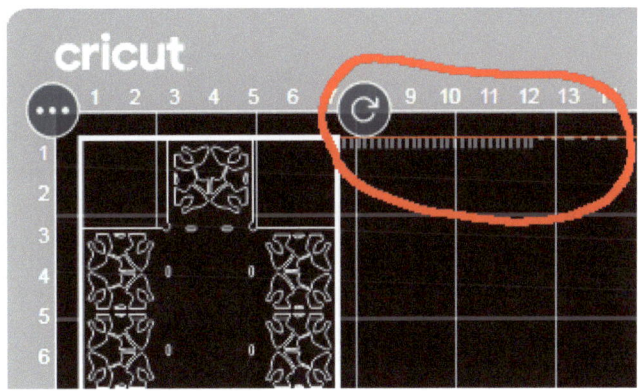

However Design Space does not respect the Group function in designs. You must click Attach before cutting or it will move all elements into their own space, it seems to assume they overlap by accident. See the fold lines highlighted in red.

Losing fine detail in Silhouette Studio
The free version of the software is capable of importing bitmaps and DXF. We initially thought DXF would be the best choice as it is a vector format so it doesn't lose detail as it scales. Except … in Silhouette Studio it can. We found it mangled some shapes and smoothed others. look at the original design and the imported result above. See the general mess, smoothed lower leaves and bendy stem.

We have stopped using it now and often I will distribute a Studio3 file that I have checked myself instead.

Reading SVGs in Silhouette Studio
Simply use the free software Inkscape, available on Windows, Mac & Linux, to export the design to a bitmap. I prefer TIF as it doesn't lose detail. Make sure the design is filled black and any details on it that need to be cut are in white outline. Import in Studio and change to the size you need, then use the Trace panel to convert it for cutting. Note that images not traced will not cut, they are assumed to be there for the Cut & Print feature.

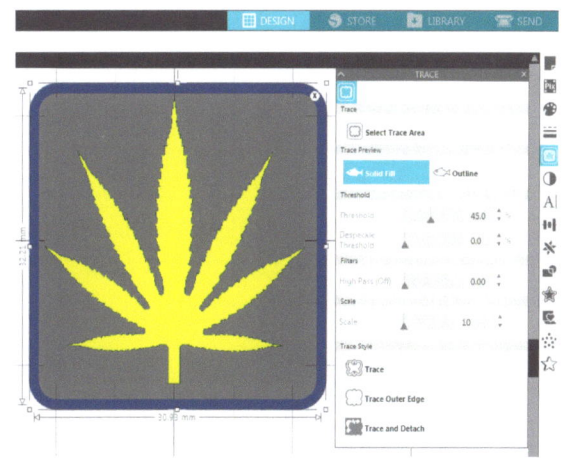

We asked Lisa for her most common issues:

Lisa Sones-Peck is more expert in Cricut and Design Space than us, and she's our go to friend and often our tester for all Cricut matters until we get our own Maker. Currently we make our designs on Silhouette and laser.

Paper tearing
- This is often too much fibre in the paper
- or it's not dense enough
- or the blade is not sharp enough
- The paper is too humid
- the mat needs to be stickier
- the material needs braying down
- trying to cut too much detail too small - we found we had to lose the details as we went down the scales - don't think the machines are infallible of course they have limitations - also the more detail you have the thinner your material needs to be.

General advice
- Not every machine behaves the same - one person's settings might not be exactly the same for your machine and materials and blades.
- If in doubt - work one page / mat / svg at a time - try not to cut everything and then get overwhelmed.
- Start with a smaller or simpler make if you're getting an odd result - go back to basics - create a simple square and get the machine to cut that - if it does that ok it might be the shape that's the issue. If it doesn't cut a simple square well, it could be the material (try a different material) or it could be the machine - try to recalibrate your blade.

Thanks Lisa!
See Lisa's Facebook Group https://www.facebook. com/groups/674621139848478
And her book Making Miniatures with a Cricut Maker.

Mix and match

It's nice to mix and match your own flowers and those sourced either made up or in kit form from other makers.

If you simply love paper, Mary Kinloch stocks many laser cut sheets of flowers and leaves ready to be made up and her sheets are not expensive. She also has videos with clever assembly tricks and painting methods and best of all for those who love smaller scales she goes right down to some very tiny scales!

If you like to play with polymer clay you may be interested in our other flower book The Dollhouse Flower Shop where we use different methods for producing flowers involving stencilling liquid/solid polymer clay mixes. These methods can produce some phenomenal colour 'prints' and have a slightly different 'look' to paper. It's perfectly possible to combine flowers and plants from each method in one scene, even in one plant. In fact, you can cut your own stencils using your cutting machine and it's even possible to cut parts from stencilled plants, but that's a little complicated for this book. We also have a book The Miniature Gardens book which has some flowers and vegetables for your dollhouse garden.

Supplies

Most materials are available on Amazon. There are affiliate links at my website on the recommended items page. These are the things I regularly buy on Amazon

- Tweezers
- Ball tools
- Inks
- Vellum
- Flower wire
- Card
- Pens

These are the things I find difficult to source in small quantity and so I source wholesale and sell from my web shop

- Paper cord
- Single sided blades
- Items I buy from craft fairs etc.
- Dental tools

Scenic scatter can be bought from model and train model suppliers and is often available from Dollhouse fairs.

Websites etc.

Angie Scarr website with links to Etsy, Facebook, Instagram, Pinterest etc.
www.angiescarr.com

Mary Kinloch
https://www.ebay.com/str/tropicalminiaturesbymarykinloch
https://www.youtube.com/@marykinloch2814
Mary supplies laser cut flower and plant sheets in Japanese paper and is very supportive of other flower miniaturists. She has a great Youtube with lots of painting gluing and presentation advice and works in some really tiny scales too!

Lisa Sones-Peck
www.spellboundminiatures.com
www.amazon.com/dp/B08QG4VY8Y

Leslie Montana full size flower art
lesliemontana.com

Biography

Angie Scarr's greatest love and therefore her skill, is in solving three dimensional problems, finding short cuts and sharing them with the miniaturist world. Angie is better known for her innovative-at-the-time techniques in polymer clay which are now part of the way miniatures are routinely made. Because Angie's experiments have often involved finding easier ways of doing things, quite naturally she's been drawn to playing with paper too and so is now finding new techniques with different materials. Angie intends to continue to experiment right into 'old age' … If miniaturists ever age! Keeping it all together is her slightly younger husband, Frank Fisher. Frank is a self confessed 'Computer Geek' who has many years of experience in solving problems for artists, craftspeople and musicians, helping them realise the digital part of their dreams.

Frank is now running Angie Scarr Miniatures at their self built home in rural Spain. For more biographical details and some of Frank and Angie's crazy adventures see Angie's autobiographical book Making It Small, available on Amazon as a paperback or ebook.

Thanks and acknowledgements

Lisa Sones-Peck for constant support and encouragement of many kinds during my digital experiments and for just being an all round thoughtful person and great fun to share inspiration and problems with. Of course Lisa's husband Rod. Those husbands don't always get the mentions they deserve.

My Patrons without whom the past 5 years would have been much more difficult if not impossible and none of the last few books would have been written. You are all my supporting angels!

Sandi Kluge-Smith, Christine McKechnie, Karin Sørensen, Gillian Mason-Thompson, Sandy Hadley, Grethe Holme Jantzen, Jacquie Hall, Marta Terán, Tara Jane Susie Langworthy, Leslie Blevins, Karen Rollinson, Robyn Stewart and, of course, many more who didn't give permission to be named but who are just as important to me. Thank you all!

Thanks to Kira. who we constantly ask for advice but tried not to ask too much of this time!

Patreon
Why I love my patrons

If you've never heard of Patreon before, imagine you could be a 'patron of the arts' in some small way helping your favourite artists to continue working, inventing and teaching in their specialist area. Artists no matter how well known in their field often have no regular guaranteed income and often give away their inspiration for free because until now there wasn't an easy method to gain an income from day to day teaching, support and skill sharing.

This subscription service is an easy way to connect artist teachers with their students and followers, and as a way for the 'patrons' to give the level of support they are comfortable with and receive in return (sometimes personalised) perks such as early access to new ideas, live patron only videos and little samples of work to help you visualise stages of work and qualities of colour. As well as advance knowledge of really new ideas before they ever get to publication. Some ideas of how I made things which never even reach the books which I call my 'daft ideas' for example how I made the awning for the dollhouse shop on the front just using parts from an old umbrella! For benefit patrons I'm also able to send out little found 'things' which might inspire you, or samples of my new tools before they go into full production.

Many thanks to my current 70+ patrons some of who have been with me for several years now. You've all given me courage to start with new things like this book. The Patreon thing has really helped me because it's like having 70 sets of shoulders to lean on. 70 therapists and 70 special friends to share my daft ideas with and see if they work. Or at least are interesting enough for you not to walk away! 70 people who understand that no matter how well known an artist is they still may struggle from time to time. That's worth so much!

www.patreon.com/angie_scarr

Making Miniature Food & Market Stalls

Angie's first book Published by Guild of Master Craftsman Publications. A bestselling introduction to making polymer clay miniature food. This is an updated edition.

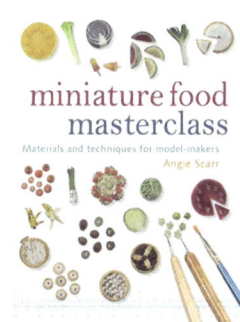

Miniature Food Masterclass

Angie's second book with GMC. Also still a bestseller this one continues the journey of exploration into what polymer clay can replicate.

Other books by Sliding Scale

Simple Mold Making
A book full of quick molding ideas for miniaturists, model makers, animators and jewellers using 2 part (Silicone) mold material.

The Dollhouse Flower Shop
This book concentrates on the innovative idea of stencilling flowers in polymer clay/liquid clay mix. Some equipment and materials are needed to get started.

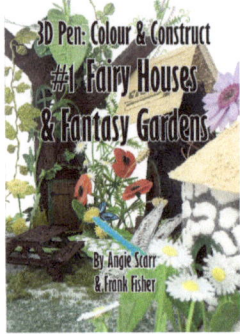

3D Pen #1 Fairy Houses and Fantasy Gardens
A handy pattern book for anyone of any age who is looking for a project to make with their 3D pen. Excellent addition to a 3D pen gift.

Your Creative Business
Angie and SEO expert Kira share advice on all aspects of craft business from pricing and marketing through to multiple income streams to help you ensure a more secure future.

Your Creative Business Workbook
To go with the main book or as a stand alone. This workbook helps you decide on your business direction and includes ideas to improve your planning and profits.

The Miniature Gardens Book
Have you ever fancied making more than just a flower garden in miniature? Angie gives you several garden styles and lots of new ideas.

Angie Scarr's Colour Book
New large edition book that asks the big questions about colour realism in polymer clay, helping you towards work that is so realistic it jumps out from the rest.

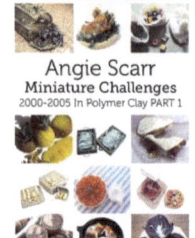

Angie Scarr Miniature Challenges Part 1
Revisiting all the old magazine articles in Dolls House and Miniature Scene and other dollhouse magazines most of which are otherwise out of print.

Angie Scarr Miniature Challenges Part 2
More old dolls house magazine articles revisited. Some with updated information.

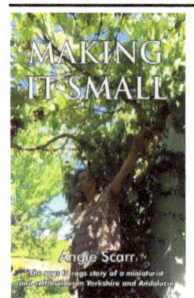

Making it Small - Biography
Angie never lived an 'ordinary life'. When she and Frank met it became less ordinary still. A story of the love of crafts, miniatures, self building and life in a small pueblo in Spain.

The Frugalist
A look at revaluing your time, living better for less and gently preparing for unexpected crises. If life sometimes feels tough this book might just help.

www.angiescarr.com

For moulds, stencils, kits, books, miniatures and other craft materials
delivery worldwide

www.etsy.com/shop/AngieScarrCrafts
Our Etsy Digital store for plotter / cutter files. Flowers, leaves, boxes and a flowershop are among the designs.

www.patreon.com/angie_scarr
Support me and get sneak previews of my work and discounts in our shop.

www.facebook.com/angiescarr.miniatures
My facebook page where I let everyone know what is going on

www.instagram.com/angiescarr
Photos of work in progress

www.pinterest.co.uk/angiescarr
Links to my work all over the internet

ko-fi.com/angiescarr
Buy me a coffee

www.tiktok.com/@angiescarr
Video shorts

www.youtube.com/user/angiescarr
For tutorials, howtos and videos about crafts and miniatures

Bundled SVG file offers at our Etsy shop
www.etsy.com/shop/AngieScarrCrafts

Use this 30% discount code for book buyers CUTBOOK30

SVG Bundle 1 includes files for:
Spiral staircase, Monstera, Grass & Twigs, African Marigold, Acer

SVG Bundle 2 includes files for:
Handcart, Sunflower, Ferns, Xmas, Spring flowers, Gerbera, Windowbox, Jugs and trugs

SVG Bundle 3 includes files for:
Shop / Orangery, Roses, Wild flowers, Caladium, Dahlia, Branches, Vines, Crates, Bird of paradise, Cyclamen, Freesia, Gladioli

www.ingramcontent.com/pod-product-compliance
Lightning Source LLC
LaVergne TN
LVHW070438070526
838199LV00036B/662